Lobacious Lobster
Decadently Super Simple Recipes

More Cathy Burnham Martin titles
From the KISS™ Keep It Super Simple Kitchens:

Champagne! Facts, Fizz, Food & Fun

Cranberry Cooking

Dockside Dining: Round One

Dockside Dining: A Second Helping

Dockside Dining: Back for Thirds

Boat Drinks

50 Years of Fabulous Family Favorites:
- *Volume 1: Starters, Sippers & Sweets*
- *Volume 2: Brunch, Lunch & Entrées*
- *Volume 3: Sides, Soup, Salad, Snacks, Etc.*

For more information, articles, free recipes, and additional titles, join the conversation at

www.GoodLiving123.com

or visit

www.QTPublishing.com

Lobacious Lobster
Decadently Super Simple Recipes

Cathy Burnham Martin

A treasured  ™ publication
Keep it Super Simple!

Published and printed in the United States of America

www.QTPublishing.com
Manchester, NH USA

This title and more are featured in articles at
www.GoodLiving123.com

Backyard lobster picnic with author's family in 1960. Clockwise from lower left: brother Jim Burnham, Grampa Hrant Gulumian, Aunt June Gulumian, Cathy Burnham (author), and Grammy Marjorie Gulumian.

Copyright © 2017 by Quiet Thunder Publishing

All rights reserved worldwide. No part of this book may be reproduced in any form or by any means without prior written permission from the publisher or author, except for the inclusion of brief quotations embodied in critical essays, articles, or reviews. These articles and/or reviews must state the correct title, publisher, and author by name.

Absolutely no resale rights are included or implied for any portion of this publication or in its entirety. Contact the publisher directly for further information.

Publisher@QTPublishing.com

Paperback edition ISBN: 978-0-9832136-7-3
Digital edition ISBN: 978-0-9832136-8-0

Library of Congress Control Number: 2017954018

LOBACIOUS LOBSTER

TABLE OF CONTENTS

	Page
Why "Lobacious?"	9
Lobster Info & Factoids	10
Basic Lobster Skills	15

APPETIZERS

DIPS & SPREADS:

Super Simple Lobster Amazing	16
Lobster Amazing Dip	16
Lobster Fondue Fabuloso	19
Popeye's Lobster Dip	19
Lobster Artichoke Dip Delicioso	20
Spirited Lobster Spread	20

CHEESE, TOASTS, PASTRIES:

Lobster Amazing Crostini	17
Lobster Amazing Mini Tarts	17
Bodacious Bacon Lobster Bites	21
Lobacious Rangoon	22
Sassy Seafood Crisp	23
Scalloped Lobster Monterey Bites	80
Scalloped Lobster Stuffies	80
One-Bite Newburgs	88
One-Bite Lobster Scallopini Rolls	91
Mini Lobster Wellingtons	96
Lobacious Mac & Cheese Fritters	110

INTERNATIONAL:

KISS Lobster Quesadillas	24
Sweetheart Quesadillas	25
Corny Downeast Guacamole	26
Lovely Lobster Tacos	26
Lobster Nachos Nova Scotia	27
1-Bite Lobster Tacos	27
Lobster Ceviche	28
Far East Lobster Roll-Ups	52

SEAFOOD & MEATS:

	Page
Brandied Lobster Cocktail	29
Crispy Croquettes of Lobster	30
Legendary Lobster Cakes	31
Crispy Lobster Balls	32
Under the Sea Deviled Eggs	32

VEGGIES & FRUITS:

Super Simple Loaded Lobster Martinis	33
Crabby Lobster Bellos	34
Lobster Happy Hawaiian	35
Downeast Colonial Kebabs	35
Lobster Taco Bites	36
Lobster Heavenly High Hats	52

BEVERAGES

Florida Lobster	37
Raspberry Lobster	37
Frozen Rock Lobster	37
Lobster Bloody Mary	38
Buffalo Mary	39
South Pacific Bloody Mary	39
Hot Hot Hot!	39
Surf & Turf Bloody Mary	39
Bloody Mary Rim Dust	39

SOUPS

Sweet Creamed Lobster Stew	40
Smooth as Silk Lobster Bisque	41
Real Deal Super Simple Chunky Lobster Bisque	42
Shrimply Lobster Bisque Bowls	43
Lobaciously Lobster Soup	43
Cha-Cha-Cioppino	44
Southwest Lobster Chowder	45

Wowza White Chili	46
Chilled Lobster Avocado Soup	47
Sassy Shortcut Bouillabaisse	103

SALADS

Super Simple Lobster Salad	47
Lobster Lurvey	48
Bacon Lobster Salad	49
Canadian Corny Lobster Pasta Salad	50
Lobster Cantaloupe Bowl	50
Far East Lobster Salad	51
Southern Style Fried Green Tomato Lobster Salad	52
Lobster Caesar Salad	53
Lobster Polynesian	54
Dilly Lobster Potato Salad	54
Asparagus Lobster Salad	55
Lobster Cobb Bowl	56
Caribbean Bowl	56
Leeward Lobster BLT Salad	73

BAKED – NON-DESSERT

Super Simple Toasty Lobster Muffins	57
Corny Lobster Fritters	57
Lobster Garlic Bread	58
Wendifully Orgasmic Triple Cornbread Pudding	59
Cheesy Lobster Biscuits	60
Cheesy Lobster Bitty Bites	60
Mom's Perfect Popovers	61
Golden Parmesan Popovers	61

BREAKFAST & BRUNCH

Lobster Amazing Omelet	17
Breakfast Pudding Cakes	59
Lobster Cornbread Pancakes	59
Lobster Bisque Strata Catarina	62
Lobster Quiche Quintessential	63
Lobster Amazing Poached Eggs	64
Lobster Omelette Ooh-La-La	64
Shrimply Crabby Lobster Benedict	65
Lobster Benedict	65
Neptune Lobster Hash	66
Lobster Breakfast Crepes	100

LUNCH – PIZZA & SANDWICHES

Lobster Burgers	31
Bacon Lobster Salad Roll	49
Luscious Lettuce Wraps	49
Lazy Lobster Lunch Trio	67
Surf & Turf Burger	67
Crispy KISS Lobster Pizza	68
Lobster Wild Mushroom Pizza	68
Open-Faced Lobster Sandwich	69
Toasty Open-Faced Lobster Sandwich	69
Lip-Smacking "Lobstah" Stacks	70
Lobacious Grilled Cheese	70
Irresistible Surf & Turf Grilled Cheese	70
The Ultimate Traditional Maine Lobster Roll	71
Hot Buttered Lobster Roll	71
Lobster Sliders	72
Lobster BLT Sliders	72
Lobster BLT	73
Warmed Lobster Taco Tubes	74
Irresistible Reubenized Lobster	74
Neptune Cakes in Lobster Cream	75
Lovely Lobster Melt	109

ENTREES
BAKED & BROILED

Mom's Lobster Pie Divine	76
Lobaciously Lazy Lobster	77
Lobster Garden Enchiladas	78
Enticing Enchiladas Espinaca	78

Super Simple Shellfish Platter	79
Chilled Shellfish Platter	79
Scalloped Lobster Monterey	80
Baked Lobster Mornay Marvelous	82
Neptune Scampi	83
Lobster Scampi	83
Shrimp Scampi	83
Scallop Scampi	83
Double Lobster Shepherd's Pie	113

STEAMED & BOILED

Tails South of the Border	26
Lobster au Natural	84
Lobster a la Rio	85
Southwest Lobster	86
New England Lobsterbake	87

CREAMY

Super Simple Lobster Newburg	88
KISS Lobster Thermidor	89
Lobster Seafood Puffs	90
Bubbly Baked Lobster Scallopini	91
Crispy Lobster Scallopini Rolls	91

GRILLED

Super Simple Grilled Lobster	92
Grilled Lobster Pie	92
Tempting Tangerine Tails	93
Lobster on the Bar-B	94
Zesty Grilled Lobster Kebabs	95

OTHER

Super Simple Lobster Wellington	96
Super Simple Angry Lobster	97
Super Simple Angry Bacon Lobster	97
Veal Catarina Perfecto	97
Wen Duc Yung	98
Curried Lobster	98
Super Simple Seafood Paella	99
Lobster Florentine Crepes	100
Mushroomed Lobster Popovers	100
Squashed Lobster Bolognese	100
Enlightened Coconut Lobster	101

PASTA

Maine Lobster Lasagna	102
Fettuccini Seafood Fest	102
Spicy Lobster Linguine	103
Cannelloni Cape Elizabeth	103
Super Simple Lobster Fra Diavolo	104
Seafood Fra Diavolo	105
Super Simple Clobster Sauce	118

STUFFED & COMBOS

Lobster Amazing Salmon	17
Surf-and-Turf Bowl	56
Lazy Lobster Stuffed Filet Mignon	105
Lobster Double-Stuffed Lobster	106
Chicken and Lobster Francaise	107
Grilled Lamb Chops and Lobster	108

SIDES & VEGGIES

Lobster Amazing Risotto	17
Baconed Lobster Succotash	109
Savory Lobster Stuffing	109
Out-of-this-World Lobster Mac-and-Cheese	110
Shitake Lobster Risotto	111
Jacked Up Lobster Risotto	111
Baked Lobster Broccoli	112
Lobster Cauliflower au Gratin	112
Lobster Mashed Potatoes	113
Lobster Mashed Cauliflower	113
Twice-Baked Lobster Potatoes	114
Lobster Veggie Sizzling Stir-Fry	115

SAUCES & CONDIMENTS
Lobster Amazing Vegetable Sauce	17
Hawaiian Sweet & Sour Sauce	22
Sesame Ginger Sauce	22
Vermouth Vinaigrette	33
Melt-In-Your-Mouth Beurre Blanc	34
KISS Piña Colada Sauce	101
Crème Fraiche	114
Lobster Butter	116
Shrimp Butter	116
Super Simple Lobster Pesto Sauce	116
Lobster Mango Salsa	117
Alfredo Sauce	118
Hollandaise Sauce	118

DESSERTS
Peachy Lobster Bread Pudding	59
Melt-In-Your-Mouth Lobster Strudel	119
Cha-Cha-Chocolate Lobster	120
Cool Coast Cheesecake	120
Peared Lobster Peaches	121
Grilled Stuffed Peaches	121

MORE INFORMATION
Where to Buy Lobster	123
Where to Indulge in Lobster	125
Lobacious Notable Quotables	133
Acknowledgements	135
About the Author	135

Why "Lobacious?"

Selecting my dinner at the Ogunquit Lobster Pound in Ogunquit, Maine

For those of us who are lobster fans, lobsters have been long-deserving of a descriptive word designed just for them. Thus, dripping with lobster's natural decadence, tenderness, and deliciousness all in one word, "lobacious" joins your vocabulary.

I hear the word lobster, and I salivate. I see a lobster or even a photograph, and my taste buds tingle! Fellow lobster fans relate, I know.

Though I had created some delectable lobster recipes over the years and a lobster recipe ebook of some of them, I hesitated for quite some time to release this new, full cookbook. Part of me believes in savoring lobster simply… no true recipes needed. Just steam, shell, devour… and repeat… dipped in warm, melted butter, of course.

Or, I could join the debate over what constitutes the perfect lobster roll. I have consumed a great many, from the traditionally heralded roll that is pure lobster chunks, tossed in a bit of mayo and served in a freshly grilled, top-split hot dog roll to double-stuffs, sliders, BLTs, croissants, lobster salad rolls, hot-buttered lobster rolls, and more! The only time a lobster roll fails me is when someone has over-seasoned the delicate meat or over-cooked it, which toughens and dries it out. Otherwise, bring it! Yum!

Finally, after so many rave reviews on a wide variety of my lobster recipes, I decided it was high time to share. Cooking lobster and various lobster dishes at home is actually easy and so very satisfying. When we prepare them at home, we also save a great deal of money over the bottom line at a restaurant.

Why pay someone else to prepare what we can so easily whip up at home?!? So, while a few recipes may have more ingredients or steps than we typically present, we're pleased to present to you lots of "lobaciousness" in our true Keep It Super Simple style!

Lobster Info & Factoids

We've been chomping on crustaceans since prehistoric days with plenty of shells as archaeological evidence. Ancient cookbooks show that the Romans and Greeks coveted crustaceans, also, as did the British. Colonial Americans were not so inclined.

Availability soared, and colonists could literally pluck large lobsters out of water just 2-feet deep. Pluck they did. In fact, often waves washed hundreds of lobsters up onto the shore! After storms, piles of lobsters on the beach were common. Lobster trapping did not begin until plucking them up by hand became less common.

Lobsters, considered the garbage trucks, bugs, and cockroaches of the sea, were served daily to indentured workers, indigent members of society, and prisoners. Lobster was favored as bait and food for livestock and pets. At various points, people became so sickened by the constant, daily diet of lobster, they petitioned to have lobster meals limited to a maximum of three days per week. Some got their way. Others endured daily lobster "cruel and unusual punishment" for years.

We may be tempted to say, "Niiiice!" However, we aren't actually thinking of eating it all day every day. We also think about how lobster is served today… lightly steamed, tender morsels dipped in rich butter. Most colonists got lobster that was already dead when cooked, and then it was cooked till very tough or utterly mushy. Yuck.

Reality check.

Even if an early restaurant menu included lobster, it reigned as the least expensive item on the menu. Of course, that began to change when Boston, Massachusetts started seeing increasing numbers of summer visitors, escaping the heat of the South and the mid-Atlantic states. The rest, as they say, is history.

When Maine started keeping track of such data, records note that the commercial fishing price for lobster was just $.02 per pound. By the 1900's it was up to $.11/pound and $.35/pound in 1950. Lo and behold, the commercial price per pound had skyrocketed to $1.80 by 1980. In 2016, the State of Maine noted that lobster sold commercially for a full $4.07 per pound. At one point in 2016, the price for hard-shelled lobsters hit $8.50 per pound. These are wholesale numbers, of course, and not the even higher prices we pay at the store.

Photo courtesy of Henry Perks

Debate: What date is National Lobster Day in the United States of America?

June 15. True, for many years.
September 25. Also true, since 2015 by annual U.S. Senate proclamation.
Okay, here's my take. No quibbling. Celebrate twice! June 15 and September 25 makes the perfect Twin Lobster Special!

More Factoids & Lobster Lore:

Why do lobster fisheries put large rubber bands around lobster claws? So they won't lose a finger to one of these creatures, right? Nope. To prevent the cannibalization of the other lobsters, because in a lobster tank they will voraciously eat each other. Yikes!

The largest lobster on record weighed in at 44 pounds. It was caught off Nova Scotia.

Lobsters are nocturnal and are most active in the dark.

Lobsters have been on Earth with little change for over 100-million years.

Lobsters can only survive in salt water. They die, literally drown, in fresh water.

The Burnham and Morrill Company started canning lobster in 1836.

We only eat lobsters when they are cooked from a "live" state. Before the 1800's, lobsters were often cooked after they were dead.

Lobsters tend to favor one side over the other, just as we do. Thus, we usually see they have one claw that is much larger than the other. The large crusher claw can be on the left or right side.

Lobsters molt annually when young. After shedding their shells, they become soft-shelled lobsters until their new shells harden. After molting, lobsters usually eat their own shedded shells, which rebuilds their calcium more quickly. The claws of soft-shelled lobsters have a lighter color than hard-shelled lobsters. Many believe the soft-shelled meat is sweeter and more tender, too.

Cold water lobsters, or Maine lobsters, have claws, the meat of which is plentiful, delicate, and sweet, along with the knuckles that attach them to the body. Warm water lobsters, also known as Florida lobsters or spiny lobsters or Caribbean lobsters, have no claws. The taste and texture is very good, but also very different than a cold water lobster. (In **Lobacious Lobster**, our recipes are designed for good ol' Maine lobsters, but if you can't get them, go ahead and substitute a spiny, warm-water lobster. The taste and texture will be different, but all lobster is yummy.)

Lobster meat has less calories than skinless chicken breast. Lobsters are NOT fattening! Yippee!

My sister, Deborah, visiting from Hawaii and enjoying our backyard lobsterfest.

The green lobster tomalley functions as both the liver and pancreas. It filters contaminants, such as dioxins, that remain in the tomalley. Still, just as the liver of other protein sources, it's considered to be a delicacy. Choose to partake or not, as you wish.

Lobsters turn red when cooked.

Lobster meat contains a full 28 grams of protein per cup.

Many people say that lobster meat is a marvelous aphrodisiac.

Lobsters' blood is clear and turns white when cooked; their teeth are in their stomachs; lobsters pee out of their faces.

A lobster's brain, actually a collection of nerve endings, is the same size as a grasshopper's brain.

Warm-water, Florida, or Spiny lobsters, like these in St. Martin, are noted for their lack of front claws, thus they are often considered a large crawfish or crayfish. Their tails are perfect for grilling! In fact, their firmer texture make warm-water lobsters even better for the BBQ.

The lobster's favorite diet includes clams, snails, and crabs.

Besides humans trapping lobsters, their natural enemies include the cod fish and the octopus.

Basic Lobster Skills

Skill #1, in my opinion, is selecting the best lobsters. I believe in paying a little extra to get a hard-shelled lobster versus the recently-molted soft-shelled lobsters. There's more meat, and it's both sweeter and more tender.

Secondly, how we cook a lobster makes a difference in flavor and tenderness. Steaming is less messy than boiling, and adding beer or wine to the water makes little or no difference.

Definitely salt the water, and put the lobster(s) in head-first when your water is at a full boil. No, they do not scream; they have no vocal ability.

There are lots of timing charts available. My guideline is just 8-10 min for any lobster up to 1½ pounds. Add 1½ -2 min per pound over that, but I never cook lobsters for more than 20 minutes.

You'll find lots of places with explanations on how to take apart your cooked lobster. Often, lobster pounds and restaurants have placemats to show you the easiest approaches. Start by wearing a bib to avoid splattering your clothing.

My Aunt June Gulumian loving her lobster!

Appetizers
DIPS & SPREADS

Super Simple Lobster Amazing

This Café Martin creation was first served on the good boat Miss Behavin' Too on Lake Winnipesaukee to delighted guests! It has since graced many a table, buffet, and celebration in many configurations. Originally, it was called Super Simple Lobster Mania, because it has so many crazy and wonderful applications. Everyone simply called it "amazing." We responded gleefully.

2 (8-oz each) containers whipped cream cheese (1 plain, 1 chive), softened to room temp
1½ c Parmesan cheese, grated and/or shredded
1 T prepared horseradish (not the hot spicy variety)
2 T Worcestershire sauce
1 tsp Old Bay seafood seasoning
¼ tsp freshly ground black pepper
2 heaping cups bite-sized pieces of lobster meat

Cream cheeses in a bowl; stir in all but the lobster. Gently add lobster. Now the fun begins!

Lobster Amazing Dip

Serving Option 1: **Lobster Amazing Dip**
- This is fine as a cold dip. It's outstanding as a hot dip, letting flavors blend and enhance one another. Spread mixture in 2 glass pie plates. At serving time, microwave 1½ min on high. You can also sprinkle chopped or sliced almonds on top. If concerned about dietary sensitivity to nuts, simply put them in a bowl and let guests sprinkle them on their own servings. You can also bake this 15-18 min at 350°F for a crispy touch. Either way, serve hot with your choice of crackers, breadsticks, raw vegetables, tortilla chips, pita crisps, or even pretzels.

Serving Option 2: **Lobster Amazing Crostini**
- At serving time, spread a bit of dip on 1 side of thin, crusty, mini bread toasts. Place them bread side down on a foil-lined baking sheet. Bake at 350°F for 7-10 min. Serve hot.

Lobster Amazing Crostini topped with shredded mild Cheddar cheese

Serving Option 3: **Lobster Amazing Mini Tarts**
- Place a teaspoonful of the lobster cheese mixture in the center of mini (bite-size) phyllo tart cups (15 per box in supermarket freezer section). Bake on a foil-lined baking sheet at 350°F for 7-10 min. Serve hot.

Serving Option 4: Get creative. Super Simple Lobster Amazing is delicious served in many ways.
- **Lobster Amazing Salmon**. Simply spread on a salmon filet just after you turn it to cook the second side.
- **Lobster Amazing Vegetable Sauce**. Spoon it over a favorite hot vegetable, such as asparagus or broccoli and heat just a minute in the microwave.
- **Lobster Amazing Risotto**. Seriously. Just stir the mixture into your cooked risotto, warm it up, and listen to the oohs and ahhs from your taste buds!
- **Lobster Amazing Omelet**. Use a couple generous scoops of Lobster Amazing as your omelet filling. Garnish and serve. (This is also good with asparagus cuts or baby spinach.)

Lobster Amazing Omelet

🗢 **KISS Variation:** Try other seafood, such as diced shrimp or lump crabmeat, or a combination. Just remember to stir seafood in after all the other ingredients are well mixed. Most seafood is delicate, and it's nice to keep as many showy lumps and chunks intact as possible.

🗢 **KISS Tips:** Take care if you are tempted to increase the amounts of ingredients such as horseradish, Worcestershire sauce, Old Bay seasoning, or black pepper. It's easy to overwhelm the delicate flavor of lobster. This recipe freezes well, so save half for another occasion. It's also perfect to make ahead and simply cook just before serving. Because you can cook it in a microwave or grill, rather than in just an oven, it's well-suited for backyard or dockside dining or for any pot luck.

Lobster Fondue Fabuloso

Photo courtesy of Brooke Lark

½ lb butter
2 T minced garlic
1 c finely chopped sweet onion
4 c dry white wine
½ gallon chicken stock
1 tsp ground thyme & ½ tsp cayenne
1 T paprika
3 c heavy cream
3 T cream cheese
2 c shredded mild cheddar cheese
Fine sea salt & ground white pepper
2 c finely chopped lobster meat

Melt butter over low heat in large pan. Raise heat to med & add garlic & onion, stirring for 2-3 min. Pour in wine, stirring to deglaze the pan. Stir in thyme, cayenne & paprika; let simmer till volume reduces by half. Stir in the chicken stock; again let simmer till reduces by half. Add cream; continue cooking till thick enough to coat the back of your spoon. Cut in the cream cheese; stir till smooth. Then stir in cheddar till smooth. Season with salt & white pepper to suit your taste. At serving time, stir in the lobster & garnish with an extra sprinkle of paprika. Serve warm with buttery crackers, celery sticks, apple wedges, and crusty bread chunks for dipping.

Popeye's Lobster Dip

1 round pumpernickel (or other rye) loaf of bread
½ c butter, softened
8 oz cream cheese, softened to room temp
10 oz frozen chopped spinach, thawed
1 env dried onion soup mix

1 can sliced water chestnuts, drained & diced
1 c jack cheese, shredded
½ c mozzarella, shredded
1/3 c mayonnaise
2 c diced lobster meat

Slice off "top" of the loaf; scoop out the soft bread inside by hand, leaving a half-inch thick "wall" & bottom in your bread bowl. Combine other ingredients; spoon into bread bowl; replace "top." Wrap in foil. Bake 1 hour at 325°F. Serve with buttery crackers like Ritz.

Lobster Artichoke Dip Delicioso

1 T butter
1 c canned or bottled artichoke hearts drained & chopped
1 large (8-oz) pkg cream cheese, softened to room temp
¼ c shredded or grated Parmesan cheese
½ -1 c cooked lobster meat, chopped
¼ c sour cream
¼ c additional shredded Parmesan cheese
¼ c finely diced fresh tomato, at room temperature, as garnish

Melt butter in skillet over med heat; add artichokes. Remove from heat; stir in cream cheese & Parmesan. Stir in lobster & sour cream. Transfer to ovenproof dish; sprinkle with the additional Parmesan cheese. Heat in 350°F oven for 10 min till lightly browned. Sprinkle with tomatoes; serve hot with crackers or pita chips. Makes about 2 c dip.

KISS Tip: Make this ahead up till the baking point; cover & refrigerate till needed. To heat, this can also be microwaved on high for 2 min before adding the additional Parmesan cheese. Then microwave for 1 more min. This recipe is easily doubled.

Spirited Lobster Spread
Here's a delightful way to enjoy lobster in small bites. Spreading this on crackers, inside celery stalk sections, or on bagel thins or pita crisps. It's marvelous as a sandwich filling or inside a lettuce roll-up.

8-oz cream cheese, softened to room temp
1 T sherry
2 c chopped lobster
1 c flaked, drained crabmeat
¼ c finely chopped sweet onion

1 T prepared horseradish
¼ - ½ tsp fine sea salt
Dash ground black pepper
Paprika
¼ c sliced almonds

Cream together cream cheese & sherry. Stir in lobster, crab, onion, horseradish, salt & pepper. Spread in well-buttered 8" square baking dish. Sprinkle with paprika & almonds. Bake 15 min at 375°F. (To prepare ahead, cover & refrigerate. Bring to room temp for 30 min before baking.) Serve warm. Makes about 3½ cups.

CHEESE, TOASTS & PASTRIES

Bodacious Bacon Lobster Bites
I developed this recipe in 2007 to satisfy my desire for a super simple appetizer that doubles as finger food or tapas. A star was born!

12 slices (medallions) fresh, hot lobster tail meat, each about ½" thick
12 pieces cooked bacon, cut in 1½"- lengths
12 buttery crackers (such as Ritz or Pepperidge Farm)
4-5 T favorite bottled "con queso" sauce, heated (or make your own by blending cream cheese, jack cheese, & diced jalapenos)

Place piece of bacon on each cracker; top with a piece of lobster, followed by a drizzle of warmed con queso. Serve immediately. Makes 12 bites.

Lobacious Rangoon
The mere word "Rangoon" makes us think Polynesian, despite the fact that Crab Rangoon is an all-American invention. Naturally, I like to serve up my favorite crustacean this way!

1 egg, beaten
½ c finely chopped sweet onion
2 T very finely sliced or chopped green onion
   (green parts only)
2 tsp Worcestershire sauce
½ tsp fine sea salt
½ tsp garlic powder
Dash ground white pepper
8 oz cream cheese, softened to room temp
2 c (1 lb) chopped lobster meat
2 dozen wonton wrappers
Coconut or peanut oil, for deep frying

Cream egg, onions, Worcestershire sauce & seasonings into cream cheese. Fold in lobster meat. Working with 1 or 2 wrappers at a time, place one T of the mixture in the center of each. Brush outer edges of wrapper with water; immediately fold into a triangle or fold up the corners to the center, squeezing & pressing rim to seal, preventing leakage. When all are filled, quickly deep fry a few at a time in 350°F coconut or peanut oil just till golden. Drain on wire racks over paper towels. Serve hot with your favorite dipping sauce.

Hawaiian Sweet and Sour Sauce
½ c rice wine vinegar
¾ c brown sugar or sweetened applesauce
2 T catsup
2 tsp red pepper flakes
½ c pineapple juice
1 T cornstarch
½ c fresh pineapple chunks (or canned,
   drained)

Whisk together or puree ingredients in blender. Serve with Rangoon or kebabs.

Sesame Ginger Sauce
½ c tamari (or low-sodium soy sauce)
¼ - 1/3 c rice wine vinegar
2 T freshly grated ginger
2 T finely sliced green onion
½ tsp sugar (or brown sugar, Stevia,
   or raw honey)
1 tsp sesame oil
½ tsp sesame seeds

Stir together ingredients. Serve with Rangoon or steamed dumplings.

Sassy Seafood Crisp

For each crisp:
8" flour tortilla
Shredded Jack/Cheddar cheese combination
Crabmeat

Lobster meat, bite-sized chunks
Shrimp, cooked & cut bite-sized
Chopped fresh, flat-leaf parsley
Shredded Mozzarella cheese

Brown tortilla for 10 min in 350°F oven (or in 1 T butter in skillet over med heat for 2-3 min, turning once to brown both sides). Sprinkle with Jack cheese combo, followed by the seafood, parsley, & another sprinkle of Jack cheese combo. Finish with a sprinkle of Mozzarella. Bake at 350°F for 5-6 min to warm the seafood & melt the cheese. Cut in wedges and serve.

KISS Tip: This makes a delightful appetizer, brunch, lunch, or even dinner entrée. Serve it as it is or with garnishes of sour cream and fruity or savory salsa, if desired.

INTERNATIONAL

KISS Lobster Quesadillas

Quesadillas satisfy those cravings for comfort food with a decadent twist. Always favorites of mine, adding lobster zooms them to the top of the list!

1 red onion, finely chopped & sautéed (or a large sweet onion, such as Maui or Vidalia)
2-3 plum tomatoes, chopped
8 oz cream cheese, softened to room temp
4 c Cheddar or Monterey Jack cheese, shredded
4-5 thin green onions, finely chopped
4 T Asian hot sauce (or your choice of variety)
Sea salt & ground black pepper
1 lime, juiced
2 lbs cooked lobster meat, fresh or frozen (thawed)
10 flour tortillas (8" size)
4-6 T butter (or as needed)

Combine onion and tomatoes in a small microwave-safe dish; microwave on high for 2 min. In a bowl, mix cheeses, green onion, hot sauce, seasonings & lime juice till well combined. Spread some on half of each tortilla; divide lobster meat among tortillas. Fold each tortilla over to create a half moon shape. Melt butter over med heat in large skillet; pan fry each tortilla 2-3 min per side, till brown & crispy. Cut into wedges; serve with salsa, guacamole & sour cream on the side. Makes 10 quesadillas.

💋 **KISS Tip**: Prepare in advance and pan-fry as needed throughout your party.

💋 **KISS Variation:** Sprinkle diced bits of papaya or mango over the lobster before folding the tortillas to cook them. Or try replacing guacamole with mango or peach salsa.

Sweetheart Quesadillas

¼ c chopped sweet onion
3 thinly sliced button mushrooms
½ sweet red pepper, seeded & chopped
2 T butter
2 (8") flour tortillas (or try spinach or sun-dried tomato tortillas)

1 c shredded Muenster or Jack cheese
  (or a cheese combination)
1½ c coarsely chopped lobster meat
1 or 2 green onions, thinly sliced
1 large ripe mango or papaya, sliced
Sour cream & additional sliced mango, for garnish

Microwave onion, mushrooms & red pepper 2 min on high. Melt butter in large skillet over med-low heat. Place both tortillas in the pan, so that half of each are in the butter; the other halves should be vertically back-to-back in center. Divide cheese on the 2 flat halves, followed by the veggie mixture, green onions, mango, and the lobster. Fold the vertical halves over the filling forming half-moons. Raise heat to med; let cook 2 min. Turn over with large spatulas; let cook 2 more minutes. Serve hot with sour cream and mango slices on the side, if desired.

Corny Downeast Guacamole

As a lobster fan, I love giving homemade guacamole a lobacious twist!

Kernels cut from 4 ears of grilled corn
3-4 avocados, peeled, pitted & diced
1 red onion, finely diced
Juice of 3 limes
½ c chopped fresh flat-leaf parsley

½ c chopped fresh cilantro
3-4 plum tomatoes, diced
Sea salt & freshly ground pepper
4 lobster tails, coarsely diced

Combine corn, avocados, onion, lime juice, parsley, cilantro & tomatoes. Season with salt & pepper, to suit your taste. Serve with crispy tortilla chips as an appetizer dip.

KISS Variations: Go for **Lovely Lobster Tacos** by spooning this into soft or crispy taco shells, lined with a bit of chopped lettuce. This is also perfect as **Tails South of the Border**. Simply serve steamed or chilled lobster tails or lobster tail strips around or beside a mound of this guacamole.

Lobster Nachos Nova Scotia

4 dozen crispy corn or flour tortilla chips
1 c shredded Monterey jack cheese
1 c chopped lobster meat
½ c raw corn kernels
¼ c diced fresh tomatoes, drained on paper towels
½ c diced avocado
favorite taco sauce or puréed salsa

Photo courtesy of Herson Rodriguez

Lay chips on foil-lined baking pan in single layer. Sprinkle with cheese, followed by lobster, corn, tomatoes, and avocado. Then drizzle with your sauce and immediately put in hot 425°F oven. Let bake 4-6 min, just till cheese is melty. Serve hot. No condiments are needed, but you can always offer such items as sour cream, salsa, sliced olives, and guacamole on the side, if desired.

KISS Tip: I also like to add a sprinkle of chopped fresh cilantro on top. When making nachos, which I do a LOT, I only follow 2 basic rules. First, keep chips in a single layer. Second, drizzle with sauce last. Both these steps keep chips crispy AND assure each chip has a perfect dose of toppings.

1-Bite Lobster Tacos

Scoop-style corn tortilla chips
Packaged coleslaw
Ground cumin
Lobster meat, diced
Peach or papaya salsa
Shredded Muenster or Monterey Jack cheese

At serving time, arrange chip scoops in single layer on serving platter. Toss coleslaw with just a bit of cumin; put a scant bit in bottom of each cup, followed by lobster, salsa & a touch of cheese. Serve!

Lobster Ceviche

2 c carrot juice
2 c freshly squeezed orange juice
1 T minced ginger
Zest from 2 limes
1 c freshly squeezed lime juice
1 jalapeño pepper, deseeded & finely chopped
1/3 – ½ c finely chopped
  or thinly sliced red onion
¼ c fresh basil leaves, sliced in julienned strips
¼ c fresh, coarsely chopped cilantro
2 seedless oranges, peeled & segments halved
1 lb dry-packed sea scallops, halved or
  quartered, if very large
1 T coarse kosher salt
2 lbs cooked lobster meat, cut into chunks

Place ½ c lime juice, kosher salt & scallops in glass container; cover; let marinate 1 hour in the refrigerator. Meanwhile, combine 1 c of both the carrot and orange juices with the ginger in a small saucepan over high heat. Bring to a boil; cook about 30 min to reduce by half. Remove from heat; add lime zest & let rest at room temp for 10 min. Then cool completely in the refrigerator, before straining out the solids. Stir in remaining orange, carrot & lime juices, jalapeño pepper, onion, basil, cilantro & orange segments. Strain scallops and add them & the lobster to the orange mixture. Season with salt to suit your taste. Serve in lettuce-lined chilled glass bowls or large martini glasses. Makes 6-8 servings.

SEAFOOD & MEATS

Brandied Lobster Cocktail

½ c mayonnaise
3 T ketchup
1 T brandy
3 c chilled lobster meat chunks (or tails and claws)

Place lobster in lettuce-lined or fancy stemware, such as martini glasses. In a bowl, combine mayonnaise, ketchup and brandy. Serve as a dipping sauce with the lobster. Makes 4 servings.

💋 **KISS Tip:** If steaming or boiling lobsters yourself, add flavor ingredients to the water. Try a coarsely-diced, large sweet onion, along with lemon wedges, a couple of bay leaves & a handful of peppercorns.

Crispy Croquettes of Lobster

As a child, I remember enjoying chicken croquettes with a creamy white gravy. While they still strike a pleasant note with my adult taste buds, these Crispy Croquettes of Lobster *make them sing out loud!*

4 T butter
1/3 c chopped green onions (green & white parts)
¾ c flour, with 1/8 tsp salt, pepper, cayenne & nutmeg
1c milk or half-and-half
1½-lb lobster tail & claw meat, cut into ½ - ¾" bits
1 T brandy
1 c all-purpose flour, seasoned w 1/8 tsp each: salt, pepper, cayenne & nutmeg
2 lg or ex-lg eggs, beaten a bit
1c bread crumbs (regular or panko)
8 T coconut oil
Fresh parsley, for garnish

Melt butter in saucepan over med heat; sauté onions 2 min. In a blender, mix the ¾ c flour & the milk till well combined. Pour into sautéed onions, whisking constantly, over med heat, till thickened. Remove from heat; stir in lobster & brandy; let rest at room temperature for 1 hour. Place 1 c flour, beaten eggs & breadcrumbs into 3 individual small bowls. Shape lobster batter into small patties, balls, or cylindrical rolls; dredge first in the flour, followed by egg & then breadcrumbs. Set aside on waxed paper till all patties are formed. In coconut oil, preheated to 350°F, in heavy skillet, fry patties 90 seconds on each side. Serve hot, garnished with the fresh parsley.

KISS Tip: A nice dipping sauce can be as simple as melted butter or as zesty as hot sauce, salsa, or cocktail sauce. Herbed creamy sauces make other tasty options. Adjust spices and your garnish to compliment your sauce.

Legendary Lobster Cakes

These are incredibly marvelous… crisp outside, but moist & tender inside!

2 c lobster meat, cut in small chunks
2 lg eggs, beaten with 1 tsp Worcestershire Sauce
2 T mayonnaise
1 sweet onion, well chopped
1 sweet red pepper, seeded; well-chopped

1 T chopped fresh, flat-leaf parsley
1 tsp dry mustard
6-8 Ritz crackers, crushed
Fine sea salt & ground pepper, to suit your taste

Toss lobster meat, egg & mayo together. Stir in remaining ingredients. Form in large or small patties, as suits your needs. Brown in butter in skillet over med heat, just till golden, turning once. Serve, squeezed with a bit of fresh lemon or lime juice, if desired, as tapas bites, with or on a salad.

KISS Variation: Turn these into gorgeous **Lobster Burgers** by serving on your favorite butter-brushed roll grilled till golden. Garnish as you like with mayo, bacon, lettuce & thin slices of sweet onion & ripe, red tomato. Add a bit of bite with thin slices of jalapeño pepper or use a siracha sauce.

Crispy Lobster Balls

1 c panko bread crumbs
½ c flour, rice flour, or combination
1 tsp baking powder
½ tsp garlic powder
½ tsp thyme
½ tsp lemon pepper
½ tsp coarse sea salt
1/3 c shredded Parmesan cheese

1 tsp lemon or lime juice
2 c cooked lobster meat, chopped
¼ c finely chopped sweet red or green pepper
1 med sweet onion, finely chopped
1 can water chestnuts, diced
3 large eggs, well-beaten
Coconut oil, for frying

Combine crumbs thru Parmesan in bowl. Stir in citrus juice, lobster, sweet pepper, onion, water chestnuts, & eggs. Cover; let sit at room temp 15 min. Heat ½" oil in skillet to 375° F. Roll lobster mixture into 1½"-balls. Fry 1-2 min, turning once, till golden. Serve with melted butter, **Sweet and Sour Sauce**, or **Sesame Ginger Sauce** (page 22). Makes 4 servings.

Under the Sea Deviled Eggs

6 hard-boiled eggs, shelled, halved,
  yolks removed
4 T mayonnaise
1 T Dijon mustard
¼ tsp salt
2 T finely chopped celery
½ c chopped lobster meat
1/8 tsp cayenne (or white pepper)

Set the 12 egg white shells on plate. In bowl, mash yolks with mayo & mustard till smooth. Season with salt & stir in celery. Gently stir in lobster; season with pepper to suit your taste. Spoon into a heavy-duty plastic bag & snip off 1 corner. (Or use pastry bag.) Pipe yolk mixture into the 12 egg white shells. Garnish with your choice of fresh parsley, chopped black olives, pimiento, capers, or chives, if desired. Cover with plastic wrap & refrigerate until serving time.

💋**KISS Tip**: You can substitute tuna, shrimp, or other seafood for the lobster, if you wish.

VEGGIES & FRUITS

Super Simple Loaded Lobster Martinis

½ c baby lettuce greens
2 c cooked lobster meat, cut in bite-sized pieces
½ c peeled, seeded cucumber, cut in cubes or sticks
1 ripe avocado, peeled, pitted, cubed & splashed with lemon juice (to prevent browning)
Vermouth Vinaigrette (below or use a bottled one)
1 fresh lime, peeled & sectioned, sections diced
Coarse sea salt & ground pepper, to suit your taste
4 fresh lime or lemon wedges
4 pimiento-stuffed green olives and/or 4 pitted black olives

Line bottoms of 4 martini glasses or wide glass bowls with the lettuce greens. In a bowl, toss lobster, cucumber, avocado & lime bits with 1/3 – ½ c dressing. Divide among glasses. Season with salt & pepper, if desired. Garnish with a lemon or lime wedge & an olive or 2 on picks. Makes 4 servings.

Vermouth Vinaigrette

¾ c extra virgin olive oil
¼ c champagne vinegar
¼ c dry vermouth
1 thin green onion, thinly sliced
Salt & pepper, to suit your taste

Whisk together in a bowl; cover and refrigerate up to several days. Shake or stir before using.

Photo courtesy of Francis MacDonald

Crabby Lobster Bellos
Enjoy these as tapas or appetizers or with a side salad for lunch!

½ c vegetable or canola oil
½ c balsamic vinegar
6 portobello mushrooms, stems trimmed to ½"
   & "gills" scraped out with a spoon
Salt & freshly ground black pepper
Ground thyme
8 oz cream cheese (plain or veggie), at room temp
2 c lobster meat, diced into ½ - ¾ "pieces
1 can (3-oz) crab meat, drained
2-3 T fresh parsley, finely chopped
1 tsp garlic powder
Salt & freshly ground pepper, to taste
1½ c shredded Cheddar, Muenster, or Jack cheese

Combine oil & vinegar in spray bottle, shaking well to mix. Spray tops of mushrooms & place, top-side-down on cooking oil-sprayed grill, preheated on high. Squirt undersides of mushrooms liberally with more of the oil & vinegar; season with salt, pepper & thyme. Let cook 3 min per side. Place grilled mushrooms, top-side-down on baking sheet. Combine remaining ingredients (except shredded cheese) in a bowl. Distribute stuffing among the 6 portobellos. Top with the shredded cheese. Bake at 350°F for 8-10 min to heat through & melt cheeses. Serve warm. Makes 6 servings.

💋**KISS Tip**: If you'd like a totally decadent buttery sauce, try drizzling your finished Bellos with this **Melt-In-Your-Mouth Beurre Blanc**. Oh, yeah!

¼ c dry white wine
2 T white wine vinegar
3 T finely chopped sweet onion
Sea salt & ground white pepper, to suit your taste

1 T heavy or whipping cream
8 T butter (cold), cut in 8 pieces
1 piece of roasted red pepper (sweet, not hot; from
   a jar is fine), puréed to get 2-3 T

Simmer, uncovered, the wine, vinegar, onion, salt & pepper over med heat until the quantity is reduced by three-quarters. Stir in the cream and remove from the heat. Then whisk in one piece of butter at a time until each melts. Finally, whisk in the red pepper puree.

Lobster Happy Hawaiian

½ c milk
1 c cream of coconut
1 med-lg sweet onion, finely chopped
1 tsp dried thyme
1-2 tsp curry powder
4 c large lobster chunks

Salt & freshly ground white pepper,
  to suit your taste
Dash cayenne pepper
½ c shredded Parmesan cheese
Fresh lime or lemon wedges, for garnish

Combine milk & cream of coconut in large saucepan over med heat; stir in onions, thyme & curry. Stir & cook 5 min. Add lobster & seasonings. Transfer to 4 individual, well-buttered, shallow baking dishes; sprinkle with Parmesan. Bake at 400°F for 8-10 min. Serve with citrus wedges.

Downeast Colonial Kebabs

Personally, nothing beats 100% melted butter with lobster. However, some say lobster must be consumed with just vinegar to do it the way it was back in the days of America's Founding Fathers. Hmmmm. Okay, I had to go for it. This recipe brings history forward with some 21st Century zing.

2 lbs cooked Maine lobster meat, in large chunks
1/3 c cider vinegar
2/3 c freshly squeezed lime juice
½ c freshly squeezed lemon juice
1/3 c pickled jalapeno slices (from a jar)
2 tsp salt
2 sweet red & 2 green peppers, cut in 1" chunks, seeds removed
2 large sweet onions, cut in 1" chunks

Combine lobster, vinegar, lime & lemon juices, jalapeno slices & salt in large glass bowl. Cover; refrigerate 1-2 hours. Thread marinated lobster, peppers & onion chunks on small bamboo, plastic or metal skewers, alternating for color variety. Serve on crisp greens. Makes 10-12 appetizer skewers.

💋**KISS Tip:** Serve as an elegant, cool entrée over chilled pasta salad or other favorite salad.

Lobster Taco Bites

Tortilla chips
Avocado guacamole, smooth or chunky
Peach or mango salsa
Coarsely chopped lobster meat

At serving time, spread chips in single layer on serving platter. Spread each with guacamole, followed by a little salsa. Sprinkle each with lobster meat and serve immediately. Expect no leftovers!

KISS Note: What? No lobster? No worries. Taco Bites work fine without the lobster. Or feel free to substitute crabmeat, diced shrimp, chicken, or pork.

BEVERAGES

Florida Lobster
We're not talking about the clawless lobster here. This Florida Lobster is a yummy beverage with a hint of the color of a freshly grilled warm water crustacean.

1 – 1½ oz (2-3 T) whiskey
1 – 1½ oz amaretto or other apricot-almond liquor
½ c cranberry juice

Shake with ice and strain into a martini glass. Garnish with a maraschino cherry & an orange slice.

KISS Variation: Turn this into a **Raspberry Lobster** by replacing the amaretto with Chambord or another raspberry liquor.

Frozen Rock Lobster
I understand a Rock Lobster is typically made of Crown Royal, Chambord & cranberry juice. No one said that we were typical, but you could certainly make that in a frosty style, too!

2 oz coconut rum
½ c orange juice
¼ c pineapple juice
Splash of grenadine
1 c ice
1 oz spiced or dark rum

Blend coconut rum, oj, pineapple juice, grenadine & ice till smooth; pour in a tall glass. Float the spiced rum on the top. Serve garnished with an orange slice & a chunk of fresh pineapple.

Lobster Bloody Mary

Surf & Turf Bloody Mary

2 c V-8 or other tomato-vegetable juice combination or Clamato
1-3 T prepared horseradish
¼ c Worcestershire sauce
2-3 T freshly squeezed lime juice
1 tsp Tabasco sauce
¼ tsp garlic powder
¼ tsp celery salt
Dash – ¼ tsp ground white pepper
1 c vodka
4 celery stalks
4 chilled lobster tails (de-shelled)

Make your Bloody Mary mix first by combining the tomato juice, horseradish, Worcestershire, lime juice, tabasco, garlic powder, celery salt & pepper. At serving time, add the vodka & pour over ice cubes in 4 tall glasses, that are rimmed or not with **Bloody Mary Rim Dust**. Garnish each glass with a celery stalk and lobster tail.

💋**KISS Tips:** Keeping your Bloody Mary mix separate enables guests to use it in a family friendly drink, if desired. Consider making some ice cubes out of your tomato juice, with horseradish, if you like. Offer any array of garnishes you like: lime or lemon wedges, dill pickle spears, olives, a strip of prosciutto ham, and celery stalks.

💋**KISS Variations:** Make this a **Buffalo Mary** by replacing Tabasco with 1 T Frank's Red Hot sauce. Dust lobster tail with cayenne pepper, if desired; accompany it with a cooked & cooled Buffalo chicken tender. Add cumin or coriander to the Rim Dust. Go for a **South Pacific Bloody Mary** by replacing Worcestershire with soy sauce; replace horseradish with Thai chili paste. If you like it truly spicy, go for **Hot Hot Hot!** Replace regular vodka with a spicy hot variety; add cayenne pepper to the Rim Dust; garnish with a jalapeño pepper. Or try my favorite, the **Surf & Turf Bloody Mary**. Add some beef broth concentrate. Add a strip of crispy bacon to your lobster tail garnish.

Bloody Mary Rim Dust

Bloody Mary Rim Dust

Coarse kosher salt
Celery salt
Garlic powder
Dried dill
Old Bay seafood seasoning or lemon pepper
Freshly squeezed lime juice

Combine the salts, spices & herbs in a shallow saucer. Put the lime juice in a 2nd saucer. To prepare your glasses, dip the rims in lime juice & then in the rim dust. Set aside till needed or fill with your preferred Bloody Mary drink.

Soups

Sweet Creamed Lobster Stew
Lobster stew is easily my favorite stew. Most are very milky; this one is a bit thicker and richer, without being heavy. The trick is developing a sweet creamy base and allowing time for flavors to blend. If your schedule doesn't allow the "rest" time, it will still be delicious. With time to rest, the flavors are fantastic.

3 c cooked lobster meat
4 T butter
1 tsp – 1 T tomato paste
4 c milk
1 c heavy or whipping cream
Sea salt & ground white pepper, to suit your taste

Melt butter in large saucepan over med-low heat; stir in tomato paste, followed by milk. Cook, stirring constantly, for 4-5 min, till hot, but do not let it boil. Add cream; stirring till heated through. Remove from heat; stir in lobster; cool to room temp. Cover. Refrigerate 12-24 hours to blend flavors. To serve, reheat gently, without boiling. Season with salt & pepper.

Smooth-as-Silk Lobster Bisque

2 celery stalks, chopped
1 carrot, peeled & chopped
1 large sweet onion, chopped
1 c fresh, flat-leaf parsley
1 (2-lb) live lobster, washed
2 T butter
¼ c flour
1 c milk
2 T sherry
2 tsp chopped chives (or thinly sliced green onion)
1 tsp chopped fresh tarragon (or pinch of dried)
Sea salt & ground white pepper

Bring 10 c water to boil in a deep pot along with the celery, carrot, onion, and parsley. When boiling, add the lobster, return to boil, & let boil 8 min. Remove lobster. Twist off tail and both claws, including knuckles. Remove meat from tail, claws, & knuckles. Coarsely dice. Return lobster body & empty shells to the stock pot; continue cooking for 10-12 more min. Let stand at room temp for 10 minutes; strain stock to remove the shells & solids. (You want 8 cups of strained stock.) Put 1 cup of stock in a blender with lobster meat; puree till smooth. Melt butter in large pan over med heat. Remove from heat; stir in flour till smooth. Gradually stir in reserved stock, then milk. Return pan to heat; bring to a boil, stirring constantly. Reduce heat & simmer till creamy. Add puréed lobster & the seasonings. Serve hot. Garnish with a dollop of whipped cream & some chopped parsley, if desired.

KISS Tip: While truly a smooth bisque, feel free to garnish the top with a warm lobster claw.

Real Deal Super Simple Chunky Lobster Bisque

With so many supermarket deli departments offering decent packaged lobster bisques, you may prefer to not make your own. However, making it, yourself, lets you balance the flavors and textures to your favorite standards. And it really is super simple to make.

4 T butter
2 T flour
½ c heavy cream
½ c light cream or half-and-half

Dash of sherry (Don't overdo this.)
¼ tsp salt
Dash cayenne pepper
2 c chunks of cooked Maine lobster meat
Paprika

Melt butter in pan over med-low heat; stir in flour & remove from heat. Gradually stir in heavy cream. Return to med-low heat, stirring till smooth. Stir in light cream; continue cooking, stirring constantly, until slightly thickened and hot. Do not let it boil. Season with salt & cayenne; stir in sherry & lobster meat. Stir 2-3 min just till lobster is heated through. Divide between 2 soup bowls & sprinkle each with a bit of paprika. Serve immediately.

KISS Note: A true bisque has no chunks of meat. You can grind lobster pieces up in a food processor or process the soup in a blender. However, we've found most people like the texture of the lobster chunks in their thick, creamy soup, so we use plenty of chunks. It's also nice to save a slice of the tail or a claw to adorn the center of each bowl.

Shrimply Lobster Bisque Bowls

1 can favorite lobster bisque (or from deli)
¼ c sour cream
¼ - ½ tsp garlic powder
1 c cooked shrimp, halved if large
1 c lobster chunks, cut the size you like
1 c shredded Swiss cheese
2 soup bowl-sized rye bread rounds, hollowed out to form bowls

Warm the soup over med-low heat, but do not boil. Stir in sour cream & garlic powder. Stir in cheese till melted, followed by the shrimp & lobster. Serve in bread bowls. Makes 2 servings.

KISS Note: You can use this as a dip by adding a second cup of cheese and serving in just 1 bread bowl. Serve with chunks of bread to sop up the yumminess.

Lobaciously Lobster Soup

6 c chicken broth & 2 c water
4 T olive oil
4 stalks celery, diced
1 large onion, diced
1 T minced garlic
1½ c chopped tomatoes
¼ c butter
¼ c flour
3 c half-and-half or light cream
1 c pinot grigio white wine
2 lbs lobster meat, cut in small pieces
1 T chopped basil
Sea salt and freshly ground black pepper
Dash cayenne pepper
1 T chopped fresh basil & meat of 4 lobster claws, for garnish

Bring chicken broth & water to boil in large soup pot. Meanwhile, sauté celery, onion & garlic in olive oil over med heat in a skillet for 3 min; stir in tomatoes; cook 5-10 min more. Add to soup pot; simmer on low heat 10-20 min. Melt the butter in the skillet over low heat. Remove from heat; whisk in the flour. Then, gradually whisk in 1 c of the cream till smooth. Over med-low heat, whisk in remaining cream, followed by wine. Cook just until it starts to thicken; stir cream mixture into soup pot, followed by lobster. Season with salt & peppers. Put 2 cups of soup into a blender & puree. Then stir it back into the soup pot. Reheat. Divide between 4 bowls; garnish each with the basil & 1 lobster claw. Makes 4 servings.

KISS Tips: I also like to add up to a cup of crab meat and a package of langostinos (rock lobster tails), but always at the end to keep cooked seafood tender.

Cha-Cha-Cioppino

¼ c olive oil
1 T minced garlic
1 large sweet onion, chopped
1 large green bell pepper, deseeded & chopped
1 jar (24-28 oz) Marinara pasta sauce
1 c pinot grigio white wine

1 lb cod or other white fish, cut bite-size
18-24 shelled & deveined raw shrimp
1 lb mussels, small littleneck clams, or combination
1 lb lobster tail meat, cut up (in or out of shells)
Dash cayenne pepper

Heat oil in Dutch oven; sauté garlic, onion & peppers over med heat for 3-4 min. Stir in pasta sauce, wine, fish & shrimp; simmer 5-6 min. Add mussels and/or clams; cover & cook 5 more min, just till shells open. Stir in lobster meat; season with cayenne to suit your taste. Serve hot with crusty, fresh Italian bread. Makes 6 servings.

Southwest Lobster Chowder

2 T butter
1 large sweet onion, chopped
1½ c fresh corn kernels
1 T sugar or 1 pkt Stevia-type sweetener
2 c chicken broth
½ c favorite tomato salsa
1 jalapeño pepper, seeded & finely chopped

2-3 c coarsely chopped lobster meat
½ c heavy cream
¼ c finely chopped fresh basil or cilantro
Salt & pepper
Meat from 4-5 lobster claws, for garnish
Lime wedges

Melt butter in soup pot over med heat; sauté onion 3 min. Add corn & sweetener; stir & cook 1 min. Add broth, salsa & jalapeño; reduce heat to med-low & simmer 5 min. Stir in lobster, cream & basil; heat through. Season with salt & pepper to suit your taste. Serve in bowls with one whole lobster claw on top and lime wedges on the side. Makes 4 – 5 servings.

Wowza White Chili

1 large sweet onion, chopped	4 (6-oz) lobster tails, in shells	1 tsp ground cumin
4 stalks celery, chopped	2 T olive oil	½ c heavy cream
1 carrot, chopped	1 T minced garlic	1 T chopped fresh cilantro
1 bay leaf	2 c great northern white beans	Sea salt
2 T whole peppercorns	2 T chili powder	Ground white pepper

Put half the onion, celery & carrot in a soup pot with 3 qts water and the bay leaf & peppercorns. Bring to boil over high heat. Add lobster & let boil 4 min. Remove lobster; set aside. Strain off remaining solids & save the stock. Put olive oil into the same pot over med heat; sauté the other half of the chopped onion, celery, carrot, plus the garlic for 2 min. Stir in chili powder & cumin. Return the stock to the pot & add the white beans. Let cook about 30 min. (This can be made ahead to this point, refrigerated, & rewarmed when needed.) Meanwhile, remove lobster meat from the tail shells. Roughly chop. At serving time, add lobster, cream & cilantro to the hot stock. Stir to heat; season with salt & white pepper to suit your taste.

❤**KISS Tip:** Make this a meal by serving with a mixed green salad and crispy cheese toasts.

Chilled Lobster Avocado Soup

3 large avocados, peeled, halved, pitted	1 lb lobster tail, claw, & knuckle meat
2 c chilled vegetable broth or stock	in medallion slices & large chunks
¼ c fresh lime juice	Crispy, dry fried onions
½ c heavy cream	(such as French's or Fresh Gourmet)

Purée avocado, broth & lime juice in blender till smooth. With blades turning, gradually drizzle in the cream. Pour into bowl, season with sea salt to suit your taste, cover & chill at least 1 hour, till serving time, or overnight. To serve, ladle into 4 serving bowls. Top with chunks of lobster; garnish with crispy onions.

❤**KISS Tips:** For a nice touch, toss lobster meat with a bit of lime juice. Be sure to only do this just before serving, so the citrus won't "cook" and toughen your lobster. For a spicy kick, replace the fried onions with crispy fried jalapeño slices.

Salads

Super Simple Lobster Salad

I first made this recipe in 2004 as a Super Simple lunch which I served to my husband and some of our friends while floating on Lake Winnipesaukee in central New Hampshire. A star was born!

Per serving:
2 T mayonnaise
¼ c finely chopped celery
¼ tsp salt
Dash - ¼ tsp hot pepper sauce (such as Frank's Red Hot)
½ lb lobster meat chunks

Combine mayo, celery, salt & hot sauce. Toss with lobster thoroughly & serve on mixed greens with fresh veggies & fruits on the side.

Lobster Lurvey

This is named in honor of our dear friend, Jim Lurvey, whose masterful creation it is!

Per serving:
Baby spinach & other mixed baby greens
4 cucumber spears
A few sweet onion slices & thin strips of green & sweet red pepper
1-2 T diced fresh tomatoes
1½ - 2 c fresh lobster chunks (tossed with just a tiny touch of mayonnaise, if desired)
Slice of seedless orange, garnish

On each serving plate, arrange spinach and greens in center; place cucumber spears sticking out on 4 sides. Sprinkle with onions, peppers & tomatoes. Mound lobster in center. Garnish & serve with a light vinaigrette or sweet Vidalia dressing on the side, if desired, though not necessary.

Bacon Lobster Salad

In the summer of 2006, I came up with this lip-smacking way to combine a couple of my favorite foods… lobster and bacon. This recipe lets you enjoy them as a salad, sandwich, or even as an appetizer.

½ lb cooked lobster meat chunks (1 c) (combination, of all types… claw, knuckles, tail, legs)
4 thick slices cooked bacon, crumbled
2 T very finely diced sweet red pepper
1 skinny green onion, thinly sliced (green portion)
1/8 – ¼ tsp Old Bay seafood seasoning
1 T mayonnaise

Gently combine lobster, bacon, pepper & onion. Stir in Old Bay & mayonnaise till well blended. Serve on a lettuce leaf with a crusty baguette on the side. This makes 1 salad entrée serving or 2 side salad servings.

💋 **KISS Tip**: Serve this as a **Bacon Lobster Salad Roll** by spreading on 2 buttered, toasted or grilled sandwich rolls. Or serve as a spread with buttery crackers, such as Ritz or Pepperidge Farm. I actually enjoy filling romaine or butter lettuce leaves and serving them as **Luscious Lettuce Wraps**.

Canadian Corny Lobster Pasta Salad

Whenever I'm asked to bring salad to a pot luck dinner or picnic, this combination is always a smash success. I've never seen any leftovers!

4 c cooked bow tie (or other short) pasta
3 c coarsely chunked cooked lobster meat
2 c fresh, raw corn kernels
1 c diced roasted red bell peppers
   (bottled are AOK)
½ c sliced green onions

1 scant tsp chopped fresh tarragon or thyme
2 tsp grated orange rind
½ c orange juice
3 T olive oil
¾ tsp coarse sea or kosher salt
¼ tsp freshly ground black pepper

Combine pasta, lobster, corn, peppers, onions & tarragon in large bowl. In small bowl, whisk remaining ingredients together. Pour citrus vinaigrette over the salad & toss well. Cover & chill for an hour or 2 before serving. Makes 8-9 cups.

KISS Tip: Make even more super simple by using your favorite bottled citrus or other vinaigrette.

Lobster Cantaloupe Bowls

Here's a fun, easy-to-make-ahead recipe that's perfect for a hot, sizzling summer day.

2 cantaloupes, halved & deseeded
1 lb lobster chunks
½ c finely diced pickles (dill or spicy hot are nice)
½ c mayonnaise
1 tsp freshly squeezed lemon juice
1 tsp chopped fresh tarragon

With a small melon scoop, remove cantaloupe from the skins, taking care not to pierce the skin. Combine melon balls with lobster, pickles, mayo, lemon juice & tarragon, tossing till combined well. Mound back into the 4 melon shell halves. Chill till serving time. Makes 4 servings.

KISS Tip: Try garnishing each of these bowls at serving time with a long piece of crisply cooked, peppered bacon, a chilled jumbo shrimp, and a lemon or lime wedge.

Far East Lobster Salad

1 T sesame oil
½ tsp finely minced garlic
2 T rice vinegar
1 T tamari or soy sauce
1 T finely sliced green onion (green portion)
¼ tsp minced fresh ginger (or from tube)

1/8 tsp ground black pepper
Juice of 1 lime
½ - 1 T sesame seeds (white, blue, or black)
1 lb lobster meat chunks
Mixed lettuce greens
2 T freshly chopped cilantro or flat-leaf parsley

Combine sesame oil, garlic, vinegar, tamari, onion, ginger, pepper, lime & half the sesame seeds. Toss with the lobster chunks & chill for up to 2 hours. Serve on lettuce leaves, garnished with cilantro or parsley & sprinkled with remaining sesame seeds. Makes 4 servings

KISS Tip: For a great luncheon or tapas item, turn these into **Far East Lobster Roll-Ups**. After tossing lobster in dressing, roll 2-3 pieces in a butter lettuce leaf. Repeat, using all the lobster. Chill them, seam sides-down on a serving platter, sprinkled with the cilantro & sesame seeds till serving time.

Southern-Style Fried Green Tomato Lobster Salad

I was introduced to fried green tomatoes in the 1970's and have enjoyed them ever since. They make a yummy & attractive base for this salad, adding lovely southern flair.

½ c mayonnaise, seasoned with hot pepper sauce
¼ c chopped sweet onions
1 T chopped fresh tarragon leaves
2½ to 3 c cooked lobster meat, cut in chunks
Kosher salt & freshly ground white pepper
½ c flour
½ c yellow cornmeal
2 large green tomatoes, cored, sliced ¼" thick, seasoned w salt & pepper
1 c olive or vegetable oil
1 c cherry or teardrop tomatoes, halved
Chopped fresh parsley

In a mixing bowl, combine mayo, onions, tarragon & lobster. Season with salt & white pepper, cover & refrigerate. Combine flour & cornmeal in a small bowl; season w salt & pepper to suit your taste. Dredge tomato slices in flour mixture and fry in 350°F hot oil 3-4 min per side till golden. Drain crispy slices on a wire rack over paper toweling, seasoning with more salt & pepper. Divide tomatoes among 4 serving plates. Mound lobster salad in the center; garnish with cherry tomatoes & parsley. Makes 4 servings.

KISS Tips: Draining fried foods on a wire rack keeps them crispier than draining them directly on paper towels. You can also substitute fried zucchini or yellow summer squash for the fried green tomatoes. Or use a combination of tomatoes and squash.

KISS Variation: These make lovely **Lobster Salad High Hats** to serve as tapas or appetizers. Use each crispy, fried slice of tomato (or zucchini) as a serving, topped with a small mound of lobster salad. Garnish each with just half a cherry tomato & a bit of parsley. Arrange on a serving platter.

Lobster Caesar Salad

You can always go Super Simple and use your favorite bottled Caesar dressing, but here's an easy way to go for the real thing.

1 tsp finely chopped garlic
3 canned anchovies
   (or 1½ tsp anchovy paste)
1 T red wine vinegar
1 T Dijon mustard
3 T olive oil
1 fresh egg yolk
4-5 dashes Worcestershire sauce

Juice of ½ fresh lemon
¼ tsp freshly ground black pepper
¼ c shredded parmesan cheese
Hearts from 1 or 2 heads of romaine lettuce,
   torn bite-sized
Handful of croutons, if desired
4 lobster claws & 2 lobster tails
   (sliced in medallions)

Mash the anchovies into the garlic in a wooden salad bowl with a fork. Spread and mash the combination around the inside of the bowl. Add the vinegar & mustard. Still using the fork or a whisk, add the olive oil & the egg yolk. Then whisk in the Worcestershire, lemon, pepper & cheese. Add the lettuce & croutons; toss the salad repeatedly until all lettuce is coated with dressing. Serve in individual bowls topping each with lobster meat. Serve immediately, with extra parmesan and pepper, if desired.

KISS Note: Don't like anchovies? Then you likely don't care much for Caesar salad. Even when you don't add visible anchovies to a salad, they are in the dressing. If you don't want to "see" them, opt for a tube of anchovy paste.

Lobster Polynesian
This is a Super Simple salad that makes a perfect meal.

½ c mayonnaise
¼ c pineapple juice
½ tsp each grated lime zest, honey, Dijon mustard, & sea salt
1 T lime & orange juices
1 jalapeño pepper, deseeded & finely chopped
2 T finely sliced green onion or snipped chives
8 c mixed baby salad greens or baby spinach

2 cooked 1½-lb. lobsters, shelled; claw meat left whole, tail meat sliced, plus knuckle meat
1 large ripe red-fleshed papaya, seeded (reserve seeds), peeled & cut into 16 thin slices
4 thick (¾-inch) slices fresh sweet pineapple, halved or quartered
½ small jicama, peeled & cut into thin sticks
Shaved fresh coconut or dried coconut chips

Make the dressing by whisking together the first 10 ingredients; set aside. Arrange salad greens on 4 serving plates. Arrange lobster, papaya, pineapple & jicama on top. You can cover & chill at this point. To serve, drizzle with dressing & garnish with reserved papaya seeds & coconut.

KISS Tip: Feel free to swap out items, as desired. For example, mango for the papaya, roasted pumpkin seeds for papaya seeds, and peeled orange slices for the jicama.

Dilly Lobster Potato Salad

2 lb new white potatoes, halved or quartered
1 large sweet onion, finely chopped
1/3 c chopped fresh dill
Sea salt & ground black pepper, to suit your taste
3 c lobster meat, cut in bite-sized chunks

1 large avocado, halved, pitted & peeled; cut in ½" pieces
¾ c mayonnaise
½ c sour cream
2-3 T prepared horseradish
2 T red wine vinegar

Boil the potatoes in salted water for 15-20 min, till tender; drain. While warm, stir in the onion & dill. Season with salt & pepper. Let cool. Add lobster & avocado on top. Make the dressing by combining the mayo, sour cream, horseradish & vinegar. Add salt, pepper & additional horse radish, if desired. Gently stir into the salad. Cover & refrigerate from 1 to 24 hours. Serve on green lettuce or baby spinach. Makes 6 servings.

Asparagus Lobster Salad

24 fresh asparagus spears, (tough ends removed), cooked crisp-tender, then chilled
6 c mixed baby greens
½ c your favorite vinaigrette dressing
4 live lobsters (1¼ lb each), steamed; meat removed; tails sliced

Arrange asparagus spears & lobster chunks over baby greens. Chill till serving time. Drizzle with dressing & serve. Makes 4 servings.

KISS Tip: This is nice with a sprinkle of sesame seeds or roasted cashews.

Lobster Cobb Bowl

This approach deviates from the traditional rows of chopped ingredients to deliver more of a snackable feast. Feel free to mix up ingredients to suit your taste, like the Surf-and-Turf Bowl pictured.

3-4" Butter or Romaine lettuce leaves
12 crisply cooked bacon strips
½ lb crisp-tender cooked green beans, chilled
2 ripe tomatoes, cut in total of 8 thick, crosswise slices
4 hard-boiled eggs, halved lengthwise
2 avocados, halved, pitted, peeled & thickly sliced

12 slices cheddar cheese
Meat of 6 Maine lobster tails, cut in strips, plus 12 lobster claws, whole
1 c balsamic vinaigrette or sweet Vidalia onion dressing
Crispy, dry, fried onions (such as French's or Fresh Gourmet)

Line 4 soup bowls with lettuce leaves. In each bowl arrange the other salad ingredients in groups around the outer edge of each bowl... 3 strips bacon, 2 tomato slices, ½ egg, slices of avocado, & 3 slices of cheese. Then mound the lobster meat in the center. Cover & chill till needed. Serve each with ¼ c of dressing drizzled over or on the side. Makes 4 servings.

💋**KISS Variations:** For a yummy **Caribbean Bowl**, replace green beans with caramelized slices of red onion, tomatoes with grilled slices of fresh pineapple, eggs with slices of barbequed chicken, pork, lamb, or bacon, and replace Maine lobster with 12 warm water lobster tails (if desired). For a dressing, try a honey lime vinaigrette or zesty mustard mango dressing. Garnish with charred slices of jalapeno or coconut shavings. For the **Surf-and-Turf Bowl** pictured, use caramelized red onion, grilled asparagus, grilled pineapple spears, bacon & avocado slices with your lobster.

Baked – Non-Dessert

Super Simple Toasty Lobster Muffins
Try these, and you'll know I am the total Lobster Lady! Here's how I spell Nirvana… simply serve these gems hot with butter, softened to room temp! (Your reaction will make "Mmmm-Mmmm Good" look like a warm-up act.)

½ c milk or half & half, microwaved 40 sec on high
1 heaping cup fresh bread cubes, diced small
2 T heavy or whipping cream
2 lg or ex-lg eggs, beaten
2 c diced lobster meat (fresh or frozen)

½ c chopped sweet onions, microwaved 60 sec
3 T melted butter
¼ tsp salt
1/8 tsp each celery salt & paprika
Dash ground black pepper

Pour hot milk over bread cubes in bowl. Stir in heavy cream, followed by eggs, lobster, onions, melted butter & seasonings. Divide among 6 well-buttered muffin tins; bake 20 min at 350°F. Makes 6 muffins.

❤**KISS Tip**: You could also feature these muffins as a brunch entrée with slices of fresh fruit and berries on the side. Or try them as a main dish with some wild rice and a green vegetable or salad.

Corny Lobster Fritters
Try these as a side with a steak or chicken dinner. Naturally, they are great on their own, too!

1 c finely diced sweet onion, microwaved 60 sec
1 c finely diced sweet red pepper, microwaved 30 sec
2 c cooked lobster meat, diced to ½ - ¾"
1 c corn kernels (fresh or frozen, thawed)
1 tsp minced garlic

2 lg or ex-lg eggs, beaten
¼ c milk or half-and-half
¼ c chopped fresh parsley
½ tsp salt
½ tsp black or white pepper
1 T chili garlic paste
1 c flour
3 T baking powder
Coconut or peanut oil

Combine onion, sweet pepper, lobster, corn, garlic, eggs, milk, parsley, salt, pepper & garlic paste. Combine flour & baking powder; stir into lobster. Using small spoon, shape batter into 1½" balls, setting aside on waxed paper until all fritters are formed. Drop into 350°F oil in a deep, heavy saucepan or fryer. Cook 3-4 min, turning with slotted spoon till golden. Drain on paper towels. Makes 6-8 servings.

❤**KISS Tips**: These can be made ahead of time and stored, covered in the refrigerated until needed. Then simply heat at 400°F for 10 min. Serve with plain cocktail sauce or 1 c of sauce to which you have added 2 T prepared horseradish, 2 T chopped fresh parsley, 2 T lemon juice & a dash of hot sauce.

Lobster Garlic Bread

In the Entrees section, I deliver my perfected scampi recipe in a manner that can be baked on its own or served over linguini. Then I thought about how delightful that would be in a crusty pastry, such as phyllo. Naturally, folding it into fresh, hot bread decadently followed!

6 T butter
1 – 1½ T finely minced garlic
¼ c finely diced sweet red pepper
2 T dry onion soup mix
Sea salt & ground white pepper, to suit your taste
¼ - ½ tsp cayenne pepper, optional
1 tube refrigerated pizza dough
2 c chopped lobster meat
¾ - 1 c shredded or shaved Parmesan cheese
¼ - ½ c chopped fresh, flat-leaf parsley
1-2 T melted butter

Melt butter in skillet over med heat; sauté garlic & red pepper for 2 min. Remove from heat & stir in soup mix & seasonings. Stir in lobster & let cool to room temp. Meanwhile, unroll the pizza dough, using a rolling pin to flatten and spread it out a bit. Distribute lobster garlic mixture over the dough, leaving a ½"- border on all sides. Sprinkle with the cheese & parsley. Then roll up from a long side, jelly roll-style. Place on a buttered cookie sheet. Loosely tent with foil & bake 8-10 min at 400°F. Remove foil & brush with melted butter. Let cook 6-8 more min till golden. Let cool at room temp for 5 min before cutting into 6-8 slices.

KISS Tip: For more of an entrée serving on its own or as the seafood part of surf & turf, cut in 4-6 slices. As an entrée, this is also nice when you include about 1 c thinly sliced fresh button mushrooms with the garlic & red pepper.

Wendifully Orgasmic Triple Cornbread Pudding

This delectable delicacy comes from my dear friend, Wendy Tirollo. She'd made her Triple Corn Bread Pudding for years. For this book, we added mouth-watering lobaciousness. Yikes!!!

16-oz sour cream
¼ tsp nutmeg
½ tsp vanilla extract
2 ex-large eggs, beaten well
2 c frozen Mexicali corn kernels
  (or 2 c corn & ½ - ¾ c finely diced sweet red pepper)
1 can (14.5-oz) creamed corn
½ - 1 c finely diced red onion
2-3 c diced or chopped lobster meat
6 T melted butter
1 (8.5-oz) box Jiffy corn muffin or bread mix

Whisk sour cream, nutmeg & vanilla into the eggs. Stir in all corn, onion & lobster, followed by butter, then the corn muffin mix. Pour into a well-buttered 9x13" baking dish; bake at 350°F for 40-45 min (for creamy spoonable bread pudding) or 60 min for melt-in-your-mouth squares. Serve hot with softened butter. Makes 12 servings. (Or make 18 in buttered muffin tins, baked 20 min for spoon pudding or 30-40 min for muffins.)

💋**KISS Tip:** Try this as a perfectly lobacious side dish for entrees like salmon, chicken, pork, ribs, or steak. Turn this sweetness to savory by adding any or all of the following: ½ - 1 c crumbled cooked bacon, 1 or 2 T dried onion soup mix, and/or ½ c finely diced green bell pepper. Top with 1½ c shredded Cheddar or Colby-Jack cheese for the last 5 min of baking time. Or, for a sweet treat, **Peachy Lobster Bread Pudding**, replace the Mexicali corn with 2 c diced or sliced sweet peaches, and add 2 packets Stevia or other sweetener and 1 c coarsely chopped pecans. Serve with whipped cream! Any unlikely leftover spoon pudding (sweet or savory) can be refrigerated and then molded into **Breakfast Pudding Cakes**. Simply brown quickly in butter in a skillet. (And these freeze beautifully.) With or without the kernels, you can use the raw batter to slowly brown in butter some mini or regular **Lobster Cornbread Pancakes** that caramelize beautifully on the edges.

Cheesy Lobster Biscuits

I've long loved the hot biscuits at the Red Lobster restaurant chain, even when they're just knock-offs we make at home. So, it made sense to me to develop a way to put the lobster in the Red Lobster-style biscuits!

2 c Bisquick or similar baking mix
2/3 c milk

1¼ c shredded cheddar cheese
1 c chopped lobster meat

Mix together; drop by spoonfuls on buttered baking sheet. Bake 10 min at 450°F till golden. Before removing from baking sheet, brush tops with a mixture of:

½ c melted butter
1 T garlic powder

1 T finely chopped fresh parsley
1 tsp seasoned salt

Serve warm. Makes 10-12 biscuits.

KISS Note: For **Cheesy Lobster Bitty Bites**, a delightful melt-in-your-mouth appetizer, simply bake these as tiny spoonfuls to get 2-3 dozen bitty biscuit bites. Bake them at 425°F for just 8 min.

Mom's Perfect Popovers

This is literally the recipe my mother made for us back in the 1950's and 60's… and the one I've used ever since. They pair beautifully with creamy lobster dishes, such as **Super Simple Lobster Newburg** (p. 88) and the **Mushroomed Lobster Popovers** (p. 100), of course. Simply slice open the hot popovers & fill with your yummy lobster, allowing filling to spill out onto your plate or bowl.

1 c flour
¼ tsp salt
1 c milk
2 large eggs

Grease pans thoroughly with solid shortening or butter; grease top of pan also because popovers are likely to hang over tops of cups. Preheat oven to 400°F, with the greased pan inside—it should be sizzling hot when you pour in the batter. Sift flour & salt into bowl. Add milk & eggs; beat with rotary beater just until batter appears to be well mixed. (This won't take very long.) Ladle or pour batter into the prepared cups, having each one no more than 2/3 full. (It's better to under fill than overfill them to avoid a mess in the oven.) Bake 35 mins or till popovers are puffed & very brown. Remove popovers from baking pan immediately; serve hot.

KISS Notes: Definitely serve side popovers with plenty of lush, soft butter or even honey butter. At a funky new restaurant called Cabonnay, that opened in 2017 in Manchester, New Hampshire, I enjoyed a marvelous appetizer popover with cheese on top. While it seems that they cook theirs on a flat grill surface, it works perfectly in traditional popover pan cups, too. For **Golden Parmesan Popovers**, before placing the hot tray of batter in the oven, sprinkle a T of freshly shredded Parmesan cheese on top of each cup. Bake as usual.

Breakfast & Brunch

Lobster Bisque Strata Catarina

I first created this simple, scrumptious dish for a family holiday brunch. They took their first bites, and eyes opened wide. Smiles emerged, and compliments rang out from every corner. Oh, yeah… This will make you a big winner with a GREAT brunch or light summer supper, served with a fresh fruit salad and crispy bread sticks.

12 slices rye bread, cubed (crusts or not)
2 c (8 oz) shredded sharp cheddar cheese
1 lb very thin fresh asparagus, tough ends removed; cut tender stalks into 1" pieces
1 lb king crabmeat (frozen AOK)
1 - 1½ lbs lobster meat
2½ c lobster bisque (deli, homemade, or canned)
8 lg or ex-lg eggs
1 - 2 c chopped sweet onion
1/3 – ½ c fresh parsley, chopped
1 tsp paprika
½ tsp ground white pepper

Place half the bread in well-buttered 13x9" (3-qt) casserole; top with cheese, asparagus & seafood, then remaining bread. In large bowl, beat together remaining ingredients; pour over casserole. Let stand 10-15 min at room temp. (Or cover with plastic wrap & refrigerate overnight. Let sit at room temp 15-30 min before baking.) Bake at 325°F, uncovered, for 45 min or knife inserted in center comes out clean. Makes 6-8 servings.

💋 **KISS Tips**: A super twist includes a cup or 2 of very thinly sliced fresh mushrooms, sautéed in butter. Add with lobster. For the holidays, along with the sweet onion, add ½ c each of finely chopped green pepper & sweet red pepper for a festive look… and flavor. (Of course, this is yummy at any time of the year.)

Lobster Quiche Quintessential

½ c finely chopped sweet onions
4 T butter
1 c diced thin asparagus spears, tough ends removed
½ tsp salt
¼ tsp pepper
2 c diced lobster meat

3 lg or ex-lg eggs, beaten
1 T tomato paste
10" pastry pie shell
2 c half-and-half cream
¼ tsp ground nutmeg
1-2 T sherry
½ c shredded Gruyere or Swiss cheese

Sauté onions in butter over med heat for 2 min; add asparagus; sauté 2 more min. Season with salt & pepper; remove from heat. Stir in lobster. In a bowl, combine eggs & tomato paste; stir in cream, nutmeg & sherry; set aside. Bake empty pastry shell at 400°F for 8 min. Remove from oven, sprinkle lobster mixture in bottom of pastry; top with cheese. Pour egg & cream mixture over it all. Return to oven; lower temp to 350°F; bake 30-40 min. Quiche is done when filling is set & wooden toothpick inserted in center comes out nearly clean. Let rest at room temp for 5 min before slicing.

Lobster Amazing Poached Eggs

4 c baby spinach leaves, rinsed & patted dry
4 large, ripe, red tomatoes, halved
Salt & freshly ground black pepper

8 poached eggs
1 recipe **Super Simple Lobster Amazing**
Fresh parsley or thyme leaves

Place ½ c spinach on each of 8 serving plates (or a large platter). Top with a tomato half, cut-side up; season them with salt & pepper. Place a hot, poached egg on top & pour a couple generous scoops of hot Super Simple Lobster Amazing over the top, letting it pour over the sides nicely. Garnish with parsley or thyme.

KISS Tip: Try serving these with some crispy hash browns or potato nuggets & a hot chive biscuit with plenty of softened butter. For lunch, replace hash browns with crunchy onion rings or French fries. It's also great to top each serving with a big slice (or medallion) of lobster tail or a lobster claw.
The **Super Simple Lobster Amazing** recipe is on page 16.

Lobster Omelette Ooh-la-la

For each omelette:
2 T sour cream
1 T Dijon mustard, country style or smooth
½ tsp fresh lemon juice
2 lg eggs, beaten with 2 T water
1 T thinly sliced green onion (green portion)
1 tsp fresh tarragon, minced (or a pinch of dried)

1 T butter
Salt & freshly ground black pepper, to suit your taste
¼ c shredded cheddar or Monterey Jack cheese
½ c lobster meat, cut in ½ to ¾ inch pieces
1 lobster claw or a slice of tail meat, for garnish
Small cluster green seedless grapes, for garnish

Whisk together the sour cream, mustard & lemon juice; set aside. Into the beaten eggs, whisk in the green onion & tarragon; season with salt & pepper. Melt butter in preheated skillet over med heat; pour in egg mixture; sprinkle cheese over entire omelette; let cook 1 min. Dot sour cream mixture over half the omelette; top with cut lobster meat. Fold unfilled portion of omelette over filling; garnish with the reserved lobster and grapes.

Shrimply Crabby Lobster Benedict

2 T olive oil
½ c finely chopped sweet onion
½ c finely chopped sweet red pepper
2 T sherry
1 c crabmeat, cartilage removed
1 c diced lobster meat
1 c diced, cooked jumbo shrimp
½ - 1 tsp Old Bay, lemon pepper, or other seafood seasoning
2 T chopped flat-leaf parsley
1 T finely chopped chives or green onion (green portions)
1/3 c mayonnaise
1 c finely-cut, fresh, white bread crumbs
3 split, toasted & buttered English muffins
6 T butter
2 handfuls baby Spinach leaves
6 eggs, poached
1 c warm Hollandaise sauce

Sauté onion & red pepper in the olive oil in a skillet over med heat. Stir in sherry to deglaze the pan. In a bowl, combine seafood, seasonings, herbs, chives, mayonnaise & crumbs. Stir in the sautéed veggie mixture. Form into 6 patties. Then melt the butter in the skillet over med heat; cook the cakes 3-4 min per side till golden. Place a few baby spinach leaves on the cut sides of each English muffin half. Top each muffin half with a cake, followed by a poached egg. Drizzle Hollandaise sauce over each & serve immediately. Makes 3 servings of 2 cakes each.

💋**KISS Tip:** Of course, you can make these purely **Lobster Benedict**, by simply replacing the seafood cakes with chunks of lobster meat! For extra decadence use the **Legendary Lobster Cakes** on page 31. You can also use a thick lobster bisque in place of Hollandaise sauce, if you'd like.

Neptune Lobster Hash

I love crispy corned beef hash with breakfast. Upgrading this traditional favorite with some lush lobster just makes sense. Try it with boiled, unpeeled, small red new potatoes instead of sweet ones, too!

2 c diced cooked sweet potatoes	½ tsp paprika
½ - ¾ c diced raw, extra thick bacon	1 lb cooked lobster meat in ¾ to 1" pieces
1 lg sweet onion, (1 c diced)	Coarse sea salt or Kosher salt
1 small sweet red pepper (½ c diced)	Freshly ground black pepper
½ tsp dried crushed thyme	2 green onions (green portions), thinly sliced

 Place warm diced potatoes in a bowl. Cook bacon in large skillet over med heat till crisp. Remove pan from heat; use slotted spoon to remove bacon from pan, leaving fat in the pan. Add bacon to the potatoes. Return skillet to med heat; sauté onion & pepper in bacon drippings for 5 min. Stir in thyme & paprika; remove from heat. Stir the potatoes into the skillet mixture. Mix in lobster; season with salt & pepper, to suit your taste. Or press mixture into 4 patties, wrap in plastic wrap; refrigerate until ready to cook. Cook lobster hash patties in butter in a pre-heated skillet over med-high heat just 2-3 min per side till brown & crispy. Turn with a spatula. Serve hot, sprinkled with green onions. Makes 4 servings.

💋 **KISS Tips**: These are great served as a side dish with breakfast. You can also top each cooked patty with a fried or poached egg for a full breakfast or brunch entrée. If topping with egg, sprinkle the green onions on top of the eggs. For appetizers, form hash into wee, 2-bite patties.

Lunch – Pizza & Sandwiches

Lazy Lobster Lunch Trio

Left-over veggies OR sautéed sliced onions,
 broccoli florets, diced sweet red peppers,
 & mixture of yellow & zucchini squash slices
Lobster meat chunks
Portobello mushroom caps,
 with "gills" scraped out
Light, mild cheese, such as Mascarpone or
 shredded Monterey Jack or Muenster

(We suggest scraping out the mushroom's "gills" since they create a strong-flavored dark liquid that some people find overpowering.)

Combine veggies & lobster. Pile onto mushroom cap. Top with cheese. Pop into a closed grill or med-low 300-325°F oven for 5-6 min to melt the cheese and warm the lobster meat. Serve with deli or homemade potato salad and fresh fruit salad.

Surf & Turf Burger

2 T butter
2 thin slices red onion
1 lobster tail, sliced in half or thirds, lengthwise
1 ground beef burger
1 thin slice of brie or mozzarella
1-2 T mayonnaise, seasoned with chopped chives, ground pepper & a dash of tarragon
Grilled split bun
Garnishes, such as sliced avocado, roasted red pepper, crisp bacon, and/or corn salsa

Melt butter in skillet over med-low heat; cook onion till soft and caramelized; stir in lobster just to warm it. Meanwhile, in the same skillet, cook burger to desired level, topping with cheese to melt it. Spread bottom half of bun with seasoned mayo. Top with cheeseburger then the lobster-onion mixture. Serve with your choice of garnishes and the top of the grilled bun.

Crispy KISS Lobster Pizza

For each pizza:
1 flour tortilla (10")
1 tsp softened butter
Dash garlic powder
2 T grated Parmesan cheese

1 small tomato, diced (or ¼ - 1/3 c drained diced canned tomatoes)
2 T julienne strips of fresh basil leaves
1/3 – ½ c chunks (½ – ¾") cooked lobster meat
½ c grated cheeses (mozzarella & Romano)

Spread butter over top of tortilla & sprinkle with garlic powder to suit your taste, followed by the Parmesan, tomatoes & basil. Distribute lobster over pizza & sprinkle cheese blend over the top. Place on pizza pan, coated with cooking spray & sprinkled lightly with freshly ground black pepper & coarse sea or kosher salt. Bake at 450°F for just 4-5 min. Cut in 8 wedges & serve hot.

KISS Tip: Enjoy this for lunch, as an entrée, or to share as an appetizer or tapas. Use a pita bread round (halved to make 2 round discs) or other pizza crust, as desired.

Lobster Wild Mushroom Pizza

½ pkg frozen puff pastry, thawed
1 large egg, beaten
2 T butter
3-4 oz fresh shiitake mushrooms, sliced, stems removed
3-4 oz fresh oyster mushrooms, sliced
1 green onion, thinly sliced (green & white parts)

1/3 c dry white wine
1 T chopped fresh thyme
¼ tsp salt
¼ tsp ground black or white pepper
¼ c whipping cream
1 lobster tail (8-10 oz), shelled, thinly sliced
½ c shredded Mozzarella cheese

Roll out puff pastry on lightly floured surface to 12x15" rectangle; transfer to ungreased baking sheet. Cut 1" inch strip from all 4 sides; brush bottom of strips with the beaten egg. Place strips egg-side down around edges of pastry rectangle to form a raised crust; brush outer edges with egg to help seal. Prick center of pastry several times with tines of a fork. Bake 13-15 min at 400°F. Meanwhile, melt butter in large nonstick skillet over med-high heat. Sauté mushrooms 3 min. Then stir in green onion, wine, thyme, salt & pepper. Cook till liquid is absorbed. Stir in cream for 1 min. Spread mixture over baked pastry; top with lobster; sprinkle with cheese. Bake just 5 min at 400°F to melt cheese. Makes 4 servings.

Open-Faced Lobster Sandwich

As devoted as I am to a traditional lobster roll, I also love lobster and mushrooms. Using a Portobello cap as the sandwich base proved to be a perfect pairing.

2-3 c cooked Maine lobster meat, cut in bite-sized pieces
1-2 T lemon juice
2 T mayonnaise
½ tsp sea salt
¼ - ½ tsp freshly ground pepper
4 lg portobello mushroom caps (no stems), gills scraped out; caps lined with lettuce leaf
2 T thinly sliced green onions, as an optional garnish

Combine lobster, lemon juice, mayo, salt & pepper. Cover; let stand at room temp 15 min. Divide among lettuce-lined mushroom caps, mounding filling on top. Sprinkle with green onions, if desired. Makes 4 appetizers or 2 lunch servings.

KISS Note: You can serve this sandwich on an open croissant or toasty half roll, rather than a portobello. Any way you serve it, this is wonderful served with a variety of fresh fruits and berries.

KISS Variation: This is great as a **Toasty Open Faced Lobster Sandwich**. Substitute 1 T extra virgin olive oil for the mayonnaise. Microwave the unfilled mushroom caps on high for 1 min. Mound filling on top; microwave 1 minute more. You can also sprinkle them with a shredded Monterey Jack or other cheese of your preference before microwaving.

Lip-Smackin' "Lobstah" Stacks
Those of us from New England are often noted for not pronouncing the letter "r" at the ends of words, thus turning lobster into lobstah.

2 c (1 lb) coarsely chopped lobster meat
1-2 T mayonnaise
6 English muffin halves, toasted, if desired
6 thin slices tomato
6 thin slices green bell pepper
½ c crispy dry fried onions (such as French's)
6 thin slices baby Swiss or Muenster cheese

Combine lobster & mayo. Spread on each muffin half. Top each with a slice of tomato, then green pepper, followed by a sprinkle of fried onions. Place 1 slice of cheese on top of each stack and broil or grill (closed) till cheese is melty, but not browned. Serve with fresh fruit or a side salad. Makes 6.

Lobacious Grilled Cheese
Little quite compares with the comfortability of a great, crispy grilled cheese sandwich. Nothing, that is, until you add tender, sweet Maine lobster meat!

For each sandwich:
2 slices quality white bread, such as sourdough
Butter, softened to room temp
¼ lb lobster claw meat (or a mixture of tail & claw meat, as you prefer)
4 slices Muenster, Havarti, or smoked Gouda cheese

Spread 1 side of each slice of bread with softened butter & place butter-sides-down in skillet over med heat. Lay 2 slices of cheese on each bread slice. Spread lobster on top of the cheese on 1 slice. Then place the other slice, cheese-side-down, on top of the lobster. Grill, turning once or twice, until both sides of the sandwich are golden brown.

💋**KISS Variations:** Try adding a few leaves of raw baby spinach between the cheese & bread or turn this into the **Irresistible Surf & Turf Grilled Cheese** by adding a few slices of crisply cooked bacon!

The Ultimate Traditional Maine Lobster Roll
The real Downeast deal uses a top-split hotdog roll, but if you live outside the northeastern region of the United States, this could be hard to come by. If you can find 'em, definitely use 'em. The rest is the ultimate in super simplicity! You can get as fancy as you want with fillers and herbs, but this is the original.

For each roll:
½ - 1 c cooked & cooled lobster chunks
1-2 tsp mayonnaise
Fresh top-split hot dog roll
1 T butter, softened room temp
½ - 1 leaf green lettuce, chopped, optional

(I love these served with fresh, warm potato chips, French fries, or onion rings.)

Mix the lobster & mayonnaise; set aside. Spread butter on both outside edges of the roll; grill in a skillet on both sides over med heat till crispy & golden on both sides. Remove from heat. Open the split in the roll & quickly line inside of the roll with lettuce. (This is only to prevent the roll from getting soggy, so you do not have to use it.) Fill with lobster. Serve while the roll is still warm and toasty.

🌶 **KISS Tip**: If you want seasonings, we suggest just a bit of salt & pepper with the lobster & mayonnaise.

🌶**KISS Variation**: A common variation of this timeless tradition is the **Hot Buttered Lobster Roll**. Omit the mayonnaise. Use room temperature lobster, freshly cooked, or quickly sautéed in butter for 30-60 seconds. Drizzle with some extra melted butter & serve hot. (And yes, we always use salted butter with lobster.)

Lobster Sliders

Despite the debate regarding style of roll, use of lettuce, and other condiments in a genuine Maine lobster roll, many people love style, flavor, and texture variations. Tickle your taste buds to your heart's content! Just remember, you only get 4-5 oz lobster meat in a 1¼ lb lobster. I like a traditional roll to have 6 oz, but you only need about 4 oz for a slider.

Lobster BLT Sliders

16 oz freshly cooked & cooled lobster meat, coarsely chopped
½ c mayonnaise
2 T Dijon mustard
1 tsp Worcestershire sauce
1 tsp Old Bay (or other) seafood seasoning
Juice of 1 fresh lemon
¼ c finely chopped celery
¼ c finely chopped cucumber
1 T thinly sliced green onions (green portions)
1 tsp chopped fresh tarragon
4 mini brioche rolls, halved, buttered & grilled or toasted
1 small tomato, thinly sliced
8 dill pickle slices
¼ c dry, crispy fried onions, such as French's

In a bowl, combine lobster meat, mayonnaise, mustard, Worcestershire, Old Bay & the lemon juice. Stir in celery, cucumber, green onions & tarragon. Mound onto the bottom halves of the 4 rolls, topping with a tomato slice, 2 pickle slices & a few onion crisps, before the top of the roll.

KISS Variation: Turn these gems into **Lobster BLT Sliders**. Omit the tarragon, cucumbers, pickles & onion crisps. Add 4 lettuce leafs & 8 slices crisply cooked bacon, halved crosswise. Mound lobster on each bottom roll half, topping with a tomato slice, a couple of the halved slices of bacon, and lettuce, before the toasty roll tops.

Lobster BLT

I am one of those folks that loves bacon with just about anything. These two all-time favorites pair sensationally!

4 slices bread, any variety, toasted
¼ c mayonnaise, mixed with 2 T chopped fresh basil, plus salt & pepper to suit your taste
1½ c cooked lobster meat, cut in ½ - ¾" chunks
4 slices thick-sliced bacon, cooked
4 romaine lettuce leaves
4 slices ripe red tomatoes
1 fresh lemon half

Spread a little mayonnaise mixture on one side of each slice of toast. Mix the rest with the lobster. Spread on the mayonnaise-spread side of 2 slices of toast. Top with 2 slices each of bacon, tomato & lettuce. Top with a 2nd slice of toast. Cut both sandwiches in half forming triangles, if desired.

KISS Tips: These are wonderful served with fresh, hot potato chips or a zesty potato salad or coleslaw. You can also cut up the bacon, etc., and prepare these as appetizer or tapas portions on slider rolls. For WOW crisp, press panko crumbs on all sides of bacon before cooking.

KISS Variation: Go for the **Lobster BLT Salad** by putting lettuce leaves on the plate first and mounding the lobster on top. Then tuck tomato slices (or cherry tomato halves) & half bacon slices around the sides. A perfect dressing is a simple drizzle made with oil and vinegar.

Warmed Lobster Taco Tubes
These are perfect paired & served with salad for lunch. They are also elegant & easy individual appetizers!

2½ c lobster chunks (¾ - 1" pieces plus tail sections, sliced into medallions)
2 T olive oil
6 flour tortillas (7"), wrapped in foil & warmed 15 min in 300°F oven
1 c shredded jalapeño Monterey jack cheese
1-2 c baby spinach leaves
2 c favorite fruity salsa (such as peach or mango)

Sauté lobster chunks in olive oil over med heat for 1 min, to warm them. Divide equally in the centers of each warm tortilla. Sprinkle with cheese; top with spinach. Wrap tortillas around the filling into tube shapes; place, seam-side-down, on warmed plates. Surround with salsa & serve. Makes 6 tortillas.

Irresistible Reubenized Lobster
I just melt at the thought of biting into a fresh, toasty, creamy Reuben sandwich. Paired with sweet lobster makes it truly irresistible.

½ c bottled Thousand Island salad dressing
2 T fresh lemon juice
1/8 tsp salt
1/8 tsp ground black pepper
1/8 tsp curry powder
2 T butter
¼ c finely diced celery
2 c (1 lb) cooked lobster meat, cut in ½" chunks
1 T sliced green onions (green portion)
4 hot dog buns, buttered outside; toasted or grilled
4 Romaine lettuce leaves
4 T shredded Swiss cheese

Whisk dressing, lemon juice, salt, pepper & curry in a bowl; set aside. Melt butter in skillet over med-low heat; sauté celery for 1 min. Add lobster for 1 more min. Turn into the dressing bowl along with the green onions. Stir well to distribute dressing evenly. Line each hot, toasty bun with a lettuce leaf, sprinkle cheese over lettuce, & fill with lobster Reuben filling.

💋**KISS Tip**: Replace lettuce with sauerkraut that has been very thoroughly drained, if desired.

Neptune Cakes in Lobster Cream

The Lobster Cakes pictured are the homemade ones from my recipe in the Appetizer section; the bisque is from my Soup section. However, it's AOK to Keep It Super Simple. Use all purchased items & enjoy!!

Lobster or crab cakes (homemade or purchased)
Butter
Lobster bisque (homemade or purchased)
Meat of whole lobster claws, fresh parsley sprigs & lemon wedges, for garnish

Brown cakes in butter in skillet over med heat, turning once. Place each on a warm serving plate and surround with bisque, drizzling some over the top, if desired. Garnish and serve.

Entrées
BAKED & BROILED

Mom's Lobster Pie Divine

When my mother, Glenna Gulumian Burnham, made her Lobster Pie Divine, always from scratch, no one ever showed up late for dinner. Nor were there ever leftovers! This is her original recipe… with Mom's love to you!

4 T butter
4 T flour
1½ c milk
½ c heavy or whipping cream
½ - 1 T dry sherry
¼ tsp ground nutmeg
½ tsp salt
¼ tsp ground white or black pepper
1/8 tsp garlic powder
2 c lobster pieces, fresh or frozen (thawed)
1 (4-oz) can sliced mushrooms, drained or fresh sautéed mushrooms
6 slices good white bread (at least 1 day old is better), crusts removed, cubed & tossed in ½ c melted butter

Make white sauce by melting the butter in a pan; remove from heat & stir in flour till combined. Then stir in milk, gradually, till smooth, followed by the cream. Return to med heat; stir while cooking till thickened. Add sherry, nutmeg, salt, pepper & garlic powder. Stir in lobster & mushrooms; pour mixture into well-buttered 9" pie plate. Top with buttered bread cubes. Bake at 350°F for 26-30 min. Serve hot.

KISS Tips: When seasoning the white sauce, feel free to add a dash of hot sauce or cayenne pepper. You can also bake this in individual ramekins for personal entrée portions or in scallop baking shells for perfect appetizers or tapas.

Lobaciously Lazy Lobster

I must admit that I Super Simplified Mom's lobster pie back when I was a college student. This is all the decadence of tender chunks of lobster and luscious butter.

Warm lobster chunks
Crumbled Ritz crackers, tossed in melted butter & crisped 5-10 min in 350°F oven
Freshly chopped parsley
Melted butter
Lemon halves or wedges

Fill shallow, individual serving dishes with a double thickness of lobster chunks. Top with the toasted Ritz cracker crumbs & a sprinkle of parsley. Serve with melted butter and some fresh lemon, if desired. Or, skip toasting the cracker crumbs. Simply sprinkle them over the lobster meat and bake 5-10 min in a 350°F oven. Sprinkle with parsley, and serve with melted butter and fresh lemon.

Lobster Garden Enchiladas

1 – 1½ lb lobster meat, cut in ½ - 1" pieces
1 c shredded sharp Cheddar cheese
10-oz frozen chopped broccoli, thawed
1 c fresh or frozen whole kernel corn
1 c sour cream
2 tsp ground cumin
1 tsp ground oregano
15-16 oz canned enchilada sauce, divided
8 (6") flour tortillas
1 c shredded Monterey Jack cheese

Combine lobster, cheese, broccoli, corn, sour cream, cumin, oregano and 1/3 of the enchilada sauce. Place tortillas on a plate; cover with a paper towel; microwave 1 min on high. Divide lobster mixture among the tortillas; roll up; place filled tortillas seam side down in buttered 7x12" glass baking dish. Drizzle with remaining enchilada sauce. Cover with paper toweling; microwave on high 5 min. Sprinkle Jack cheese over the enchiladas; microwave 1 more min. Let stand at room temp for 2 min. Makes 8.

💋**KISS Tips**: Serve these with extra warmed enchilada sauce as gravy and garnish with a sprinkle of thinly sliced green onions (green portion). They are great served with rice & refried beans. I also love this browned in butter! Try **Enticing Enchiladas Espinaca** by replacing the broccoli with baby spinach, and replace the enchilada sauce with hot, melty espinaca sauce!

Super Simple Shellfish Platter

Chilled Shellfish Platter

6 T extra-virgin olive oil
¼ c finely chopped sweet onion
2 T minced fresh parsley
½ tsp finely grated lemon peel
6 very large sea scallops
6 jumbo shrimp, peeled, deveined, butterflied
2 large lobster tails, halved lengthwise
4 Alaskan King crab legs, shells halved lengthwise, other other crab legs
2 T water
Lemon wedges
Fresh parsley sprigs

Brush a large roasting pan with 2 T of the olive oil. In a small bowl, combine onion, parsley & lemon peel. Brush remaining olive oil over lobster tails, shrimp, scallops & crab (meat & shells). Sprinkle with salt & pepper and the onion mixture. Place scallops in roasting pan; cook 3 min at 450°F. Turn them over; add shrimp to the pan. Roast 2 min; turn shrimp over. Add the lobster & crab, plus the 2 T water. Roast just 3 more minutes to heat lobster & crab through. Arrange shellfish on warm platter, garnished with lemon & parsley. Pour any pan drippings over shellfish. Serve hot with melted butter, zesty cocktail sauce or tartar sauce.

KISS Note: This also works nicely as a **Chilled Shellfish Platter**. Use any combo, such as lobster claws, stone crab claws & jumbo shrimp, as pictured. Or add half a dozen raw clams. Add horseradish & hot sauce to your condiments. You could also remove the lobster & crab from the shells.

Scalloped Lobster Monterey

1 lb fresh sea or scallops, steamed for just 3-5 min
1 lb lobster meat chunks
2 T butter
2 T flour
1 c milk
1 c shredded Monterey Jack cheese
2 T grated or shredded Parmesan cheese
1 jalapeño pepper, de-seeded & finely chopped, optional

Place scallops & lobster in 6-8 buttered individual, shallow baking dishes or large scallop shells. Melt butter over low heat in small saucepan. Whisk in flour till smooth; remove from heat. Gradually stir in milk till smooth over med heat till thickened. Stir in Monterey Jack cheese. Spoon over lobster mixture. Sprinkle with Parmesan & jalapeño peppers (if using). Broil just till lightly browned. Makes 6-8 servings.

KISS Variation: Turn this into a decadent appetizer, **Scalloped Lobster Monterey Bites**, by putting seafood into baked, bite-sized phyllo pastry cups before topping with cheese sauce & broiling or baking just 1-2 min. Or make as **Scalloped Lobster Stuffies** by combining all ingredients along with ¼ - ½ c panko bread crumbs. Fill large clam shells, topping with parsley & a pat of butter; grill (closed cover) on med 12-15 min. There will be no leftovers!

Photo courtesy of Jeffrey Larrabee

Baked Lobster Mornay Marvelous

¼ c butter
1 c thinly sliced button mushrooms
2 T flour
1 c chicken broth
1 c heavy cream (or half-and-half)
½ tsp ground white pepper
1-2 c lobster meat, cut in bite-sized pieces
½ c shredded Parmesan cheese

Melt butter over med heat; sauté mushrooms 2 min. Remove from heat; stir in flour. Gradually whisk in broth. Return to heat & gradually whisk in cream & pepper. Stir for 5-10 min, till thickened. Add lobster & cheese. Spoon into 2-3 individual baking dishes or the reserved shells of the lobster tails; bake at 375°F for 5 min. (Or serve over hot pasta, rather than baked.)

Neptune Scampi

6 T butter, divided
1½ lb shrimp, shells removed, deveined
1 lb dry-pack sea scallops, halved if large
1 – 1½ T finely minced garlic
2 c sliced mushrooms (canned or fresh)
3 T flour
1 c dry white wine

1 tsp Dijon mustard
½ c diced sweet red pepper
Salt & ground white pepper, to suit your taste
¼ - ½ tsp cayenne pepper, optional
Meat from 2 lobsters
½ c chopped fresh flat-leaf parsley
1 c shredded Parmesan cheese

Melt half the butter in large skillet over med heat; sauté shrimp & scallops for 2 min only; remove with slotted spoon. Then sauté garlic & mushrooms for 2 min; remove with slotted spoon to the seafood mixture. Melt remaining butter; remove from heat & stir in flour. Very gradually, pour in wine, stirring or whisking till smooth. Add mustard, peppers & seasoning, lobster meat, seafood-mushroom mixture, parsley & half the cheese. Spoon into a shallow baking dish or individual shells. Sprinkle with remaining cheese; bake at 350°F for 10-12 min.

💋**KISS Tip:** Instead of baking this, serve over hot linguini pasta; sprinkle with the remaining cheese and a little extra fresh parsley. You can also make this a creamier sauce by adding up to 1 c heavy cream.

💋**KISS Variations:** Naturally, it works perfectly as **Lobster Scampi**, **Shrimp Scampi**, or **Scallop Scampi** by featuring just that seafood.

Shrimp Scampi

STEAMED & BOILED

Lobster au Natural
The debate rages on… which is best, boiled or steamed? I love lobster either way, but to minimize flavor loss, go for steaming, just as you would with fresh vegetables. The hot steam from the boiling water kills the lobsters just as fast as the boiling water itself. Another huge secret is to not overcook lobster! That toughens even the sweetest cold water crustacean.

1/3 c sea salt
4 lobsters, 2 lbs each
Melted butter
4 lemon wedges

Put 2-3" water in a pot large enough to hold all 4 lobsters. Stir in the 1/3 c sea salt; bring water to boil over high heat. Lower lobsters head first into the steaming pot, cover and bring back to boil. Let steam 12-15 minutes maximum. Remove lobsters with large tongs. Serve with melted butter & lemon wedges.

Lobster a la Rio

Traveling to Carnival in Rio de Janeiro meant first-hand experience of so much of what we'd only seen in videos, on film, or in pictures. The love of lobster lets you bring some Brazilian flavor home any time you want!

2 T olive oil
6 oz chorizo Portuguese sausage, chopped
1 c finely chopped yellow onions
¼ c finely chopped red bell peppers
1 c peeled diced potatoes, boiled 6-8 min; drained
2 T minced garlic
2 T chopped fresh Italian parsley

1½ c seeded, chopped tomatoes
1 tsp salt
½-1 tsp crushed red pepper flakes
½ c dry white wine
Meat from freshly steamed 2 – 2½-lb lobster
¼ c chopped green onions (green & white parts)
¼ c chopped black olives, optional

Cook sausage in olive oil over med-hi heat for 4 min; stir in onions & red bell peppers; cook 2-3 min. Stir in the potatoes, garlic, parsley & tomatoes. Season with salt & crushed red pepper. Stir in wine, reduce heat to low & simmer 2 min. Divide hot lobster meat between 2 soup bowls; spoon sausage mixture over lobster. Garnish with green onions & black olives, if desired. Serve hot. Makes 2 servings.

KISS Tip: This is delicious served with some crusty bread and a side salad.

From Rio de Janeiro, 2012 Carnival

Southwest Lobster

4 T sea salt
4 lobsters (each 1½ lbs)
½ c butter (¼ lb)
Juice of 2 limes
¼ c chopped fresh cilantro
Dash cayenne pepper

Bring 8 quarts of salted water to a boil. Add lobsters, head first; cook 10 min. Meanwhile, melt butter in small saucepan. Stir in lime juice, cilantro & cayenne. Serve lobster with the southwest seasoned dipping butter. Makes 4 servings.

New England Lobsterbake

As a youngster, I learned to cherish delectable seafood at New England Clam/Lobsterbakes on the coast of Maine. These happened when large holes were dug in the ground, which were lined with firewood, rocks, and seaweed (just as native Americans did), plus layers of potatoes, onions, corn, lobsters, and soft-shell clams (steamers). The "bake" is a bit of a misnomer, as the fire used the moisture in the seaweed to literally "steam" the food. Regardless, we can do this today quite simply over a kitchen stove or even a large BBQ grill. Yum… in any language.

2 lb seaweed
4 live lobsters (1¼ - 1½ lbs each)
4 small sweet or yellow onions
1 lb small yellow or new potatoes
4 ears corn on the cob, husked
4-6 lbs small soft-shelled, steamer clams
2 T Old Bay (or other favorite) seafood seasoning
2 c water
1 c salted butter, melted
Juice of 1 lemon

Line a 16-qt pot (at least 10-12" diameter) with 1" of seaweed. Place lobsters on seaweed and arrange onions, potatoes & corn along edges and between lobsters. Top with steamers. Cover with remaining seaweed. Sprinkle with seafood seasoning; pour the water over it all. Cover with foil and place on preheated hot stovetop or BBQ Grill.

When you see steam start to escape, give it 15-20 min. Then remove from the heat & let rest, still covered, for 4 minutes before serving with dipping sauce made of the lemon juice and melted butter. Makes 4 large servings.

KISS Tips: Discard any clams that have not opened after being steamed. Also, if your seafood market cannot get you seaweed, add a T sea salt to the water and substitute 3-4 lbs spinach.

CREAMY

Super Simple Lobster Newburg
This is one of the most wonderful ways to present a splashy-looking and tasting entrée without all the "fuss."

¼ c butter	2 T dry sherry (you can substitute dry white wine)
2 T flour	2 lg egg yolks, slightly beaten
½ tsp salt	1½ c light cream
¼ tsp paprika	2 c (1 lb) cooked lobster meat, cut in ½ - 1" pieces

In top of double boiler over simmering water, melt butter; stir in flour. Stir in salt, paprika & sherry, then lobster. In small bowl, combine yolks & cream. Stir a couple of spoonfuls of hot butter mixture into cream mixture. Gradually stir entire cream mixture into butter. Cook over lowest heat just till thickened, stirring often. Stir in lobster; cook 1-2 more min, just to heat lobster. Serve over crispy toast points or in puff pastry patty shells. Makes 4 servings.

KISS Variation: For **One-Bite Newburgs** spoon filling into pre-made miniature phyllo pastry cups; serve with freshly chopped parsley on top.

KISS Lobster Thermidor

The first time I was served a Lobster Thermidor in a restaurant, I was wide-eyed, overwhelmed by the richness and unrelenting decadence. When I figured out how simply it could actually be made, I felt giddy. Naturally, I must let you enjoy this pleasure, as well.

6 whole lobsters (1½ - 2-lb size), steamed
4 T melted butter
¼ c Dijon mustard
6 T butter
6 T flour
1 c milk
2 c heavy or whipping cream
1 c coarsely grated or shredded Parmesan cheese
Sea salt
Freshly ground black pepper
2 T butter (not melted)

Remove meat from the lobsters, cutting into large chunks & saving 4 of the tail shells to use as your "dishes." Brush insides of the 4 "dish" shells with 4 T melted butter, followed by mustard. Set aside in edged baking pan. Mound lobster meat into the 4 prepared "dishes." In saucepan, melt 6 T butter over low heat. Remove from heat; stir in flour. Gradually add milk, stirring till smooth. Return to low heat & cook, stirring constantly, till sauce thickens. Stir in cream, 1/3 of the cheese and salt & pepper to suit your taste. Pour sauce over the 4 filled lobster shells. Sprinkle with remaining cheese; dot with remaining butter. Bake 6-8 min 400°F. Serve hot. Makes 4.

KISS Tip: This is also lovely with the addition of sautéed sliced mushrooms. If you find coral (eggs) in the lobsters, you can mix it in with the cream to add to the sauce near the end. If you prefer, simply save it for another use. Garnish with lemon wedges & sprigs of parsley. For added decadence, pair with a small bowl of lobster bisque.

Lobster Seafood Puffs

1 pkg of 6 frozen puff pastry shells
3 T butter
¼ c chopped sweet onion
1 lb dry pack sea scallops, halved crosswise
1 lb raw med shrimp, peeled & deveined
¼ c dry white wine
¼ c chopped sweet red pepper
2 c sliced & diced lobster meat
Meat of 6 lobster claws & 6 sprigs of parsley, for garnish

Sauce:
1 c butter
1 sweet onion, finely chopped
1 stalk celery, chopped or thinly sliced
1 c lobster or fish stock
½ c dry white wine
2 T cream or half-and-half
1 T sherry
Fresh lemon juice, salt, white pepper

Bake pastry shells per pkg directions. Scoop out & discard centers, reserving each crispy lid. In large saucepan or skillet, melt the 3 T butter; sauté ¼ c onion 2 min over med heat. Add scallops & shrimp, let cook 2 min, stirring once. Stir in the ¼ c white wine & the sweet red pepper. With a slotted spoon, remove seafood to a bowl with the lobster meat. Prepare the sauce by slicing 3 T of the 1 c butter into the pan; sauté the onion & celery for 2 min over med heat. Stir in lobster stock & cook on high heat for 10 min, till reduced by half. Add the white wine; continue boiling 4-5 min, till reduced by half again. Lower heat to med; cut remaining butter in 1 slice at a time, whisking to keep sauce smooth. Then whisk in the cream & sherry; season with salt, pepper & lemon juice to suit your taste. Keep warm over very low heat, stirring often. Warm seafood up with ¼ of the sauce over low heat for just 2 min. Divide seafood among the 6 pastry shells on individual serving dishes. Top with their reserved pastry lids and garnish each with a lobster claw & parsley sprig. Drizzle remaining sauce around the edges or serve in gravy boat on the side.

Bubbly Baked Lobster Scallopini

1 lb sea scallops, halved if too large
2 T butter
1 large sweet onion, chopped
3 celery stalks, sliced or chopped
1 green bell pepper, deseeded & chopped

8-oz can sliced mushrooms
1 lb lobster meat (frozen is fine)
10-oz can cond. cream of mushroom soup
1-2 c bread cubes or Ritz crackers crumbs, tossed with ¼ - ½ c melted butter

Rinse scallops; pat dry with paper towels; season with sea salt. Melt butter in skillet over med heat; sauté onion, celery & green pepper for 3 min; add mushrooms, scallops & lobster. Spoon into well-buttered shallow casserole or 4 individual baking dishes. Cover with soup & soup, followed by buttered crumbs. Bake 30 min at 350°F. Serve hot. Makes 4 generous servings.

KISS Variation: For an elegant presentation, turn this into **Crispy Lobster Scallopini Rolls**, which also works with other recipes, such as Lobster Thermidor or Lobster Seafood Puffs. Unwrap a 16-oz of thawed phyllo pastry (need 16 sheets) onto a piece of plastic wrap. Top with another layer of plastic wrap or damp, clean dish towel to keep pastry from drying out. For each serving, take 2 sheets of phyllo, one on top of the other; fold in half crosswise. Brush with melted butter. Spoon ¼ of the filling in the center about 3" from one of the short ends. Fold that short end up over the filling; roll once. Then fold both side edges toward center over the filling. Continue rolling, forming an oblong roll. Brush all over with melted butter; place seam-side down on baking pan. Repeat with remaining filling. Bake at 375°F for 25-30 min. Makes 4 rolls. You could also make 8 smaller rolls, using just 1 sheet of phyllo for each. For a great entrée presentation, serve each roll surrounded with a little lobster bisque.

Or make **Bite-Sized Lobster Scallopini Rolls** for 24 appetizer servings, by cutting each sheet of phyllo lengthwise into 3 narrow sheets.

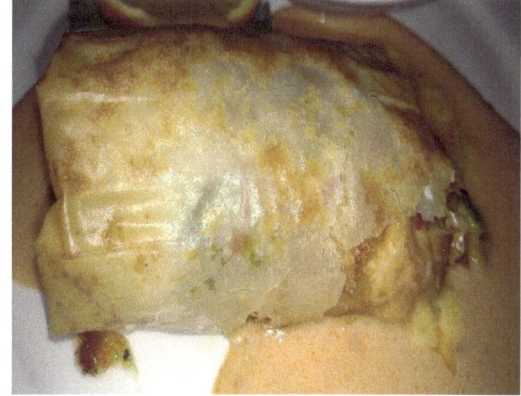

GRILLED

Super Simple Grilled Lobster
There's nothing quite like lobster & melted butter… straight off your barbecue.

4 (2-lbs each) live Maine lobsters
Olive oil

Preheat grill to medium-high. Place lobsters, one at a time, on their backs on a cutting board. Aim the point of a large knife at the point between the legs and just below where the claws connect to the body. In one move, insert the knife, with the cutting side pointing toward the lobster's head. Forcefully insert the blade and cut down, cutting the center of the body and the head in half. Brush oil over all sides of the prepared lobsters; place, bottom side down, on the hot grill. Cook 8 min for a 2-lb lobster. Serve with melted butter.

KISS Tips & Variation: To keep the lobster tails from curling during cooking, insert a metal skewer lengthwise through the tail before grilling. If using just lobster tails, simply brush with olive oil before putting on the hot grill; they will be done in just 6 minutes, 8 minutes for very large tails. Not sure how many folks will be dining? Make **Grilled Lobster Pie**. Steam lobsters; cut meat in chunks; mound in heavy foil trays. Drizzle with melted butter; sprinkle with Ritz cracker crumbles tossed with melted butter. To serve, simply rewarm on closed grill over med heat. Make as much as you'd like!

Tempting Tangerine Tails

1 c butter
Juice of 2-3 tangerines & Zest from 2 tangerines
½ tsp fine sea salt
4 large lobster tails (6-8 oz each)
8 jumbo to colossal shrimp, shells removed; deveined

Melt butter over low heat; stir in tangerine juice, zest & salt. Pour off ½ c, reserving the rest to serve as dipping sauce. Use sharp kitchen shears to cut lengthwise down both sides of the tails' underbellies along the hard outer shells, so you can remove it & expose the meat. Thread a metal skewer lengthwise through the center of each tail to prevent curling when it cooks. With the tails lying on the shell side, lightly brush the meat with the tangerine butter. Grill on pre-heated grill, meat-sides-down over med heat just 2 min. Turn over; brush generously with tangerine butter. Add shrimp to the grill. Let lobster tails cook another 4-5 min meat-sides-up, brushing again a couple times; turn shrimp over after 2 min. Garnish with a sprinkle of fresh parsley. Serve warm with reserved dipping tangerine butter sauce. Makes 4 servings.

KISS Tip: These are nice simply served with asparagus spears and tomatoes or roasted new potatoes.

Lobster on the Bar-B
If cutting a live lobster makes you squeamish, here's a way to make initial prep more traditional.

2 live Maine lobsters (1- ½ lbs each)
Melted butter (½ c per lobster + more for dipping)
Lemon juice (from half a fresh lemon)

Bring 2" water to a boil with ¼ c salt. Once boiling, put the 2 lobsters headfirst into the water; steam for just 4 min. Remove lobsters from water, placing them on their backs. Use large, sharp knife to split the lobsters in half vertically. Place them on a spray-coated grill preheated to high with the meat side down for just 1 min. Turn lobsters over, so their shell sides are down. Pour melted butter & lemon juice into meaty sides. Reduce heat to med, close grill cover; let cook just 6-8 more min. Serve with melted butter. Makes 4 half lobsters or 2 dinner servings.

KISS Tips: After you turn the lobsters over on the grill, you can also crack the claws & pour some melted butter into the claw shells, too. If you are working with warm water lobsters, this works fine also. Simply cut each tail in half vertically or thread with bamboo skewer to prevent curling. Start them meat-side-down on your grill just to get a light char on the tail meat. Turn the tails over and pour on your butter & lemon juice. Sprinkle with parsley or cilantro, if desired.

Zesty Grilled Lobster Kebabs

Meat of 2 fresh lobster tails, halved lengthwise
½ c fresh orange juice
1 sweet onion, finely chopped
1 T grated orange peel
½ tsp fresh lemon juice
Pinch sea salt
4 T butter

Cut each lobster tail half in 3 long strips. Bring orange juice & onion to boil over med-high heat in small saucepan; let boil till liquid is reduced by half (about 2-3 min). Reduce heat to low; stir in orange peel, lemon juice & salt. Then stir in the butter, 1 T at a time, until melted. Thread 3 pieces of lobster tail onto each of 4 warm water-soaked bamboo skewers; spritz with olive oil & sprinkle with more sea salt. Place on grill grate over med-high heat for just 1 min per side (2 min if raw). Drizzle orange butter sauce over the hot lobster kebabs & serve with wild rice & a fresh salad. Makes 2 servings.

KISS Tip: For a smooth sauce, strain the orange-onion mixture before adding the butter.

Author's Dad (Bob Burnham) and sister (Deborah) celebrating lobster!

OTHER

Super Simple Lobster Wellington
If you love the elegance of a crisp, pastry-wrapped entrée, you will love this. The finished product is pure romantic decadence, but it's so easy!

½ c butter
2 T finely chopped sweet onions
1 T brandy
1 c heavy cream
1 tsp paprika
Sea salt & ground white pepper, to suit your taste
4 cooked lobster tails, cut in bite-sized pieces
2 sheets phyllo dough
1/3 c melted butter
½ fresh lemon
4 small pats of butter (1 tsp each)
2 T snipped or chopped fresh parsley

Melt butter in a skillet over med heat; sauté onions for 1 min; stir in brandy. (Yes, you can flame it, if you desire). Quickly sauté the lobster pieces for just 1 min; then remove them from the butter mixture. To the same skillet, stir in cream, paprika, salt & pepper. Stir over med heat for 5-6 min to reduce.
On work surface, cut phyllo sheets in half, crosswise. Brush the 4 pieces with melted butter. Divide the lobster among the sheets, mounding it in one corner of each sheet. Squeeze a bit of lemon juice over each mound of lobster & place a pat of butter on each. Wrap the Wellingtons by folding pastry over the lobster & then folding again & again until lobster meat is fully enclosed in a pastry packet. Brush each packet with remaining melted butter; bake 20 min at 375°F till golden brown. Serve with the warm cream sauce drizzled over the top, with the rest on the side. Garnish with fresh parsley. Makes 4 Wellingtons.

KISS Tips: Kick the lobaciousness up a notch by including some extra lobster, finely diced in the cream sauce. You can also cut the pastry into 8 pieces, creating **Mini Lobster Wellingtons**, which make great tapas portions with lots of WOW factor. To serve, skewer each with a small bamboo pick & put a bowl of the sauce in the middle for dipping. Yummmm… you'd best double the recipe!

Super Simple Angry Lobster
Originally served Angry Lobster in a fancy steak house, my taste buds screamed for more! Battering and frying a lobster in its shell, however, isn't the most practical option for most of us. Our Super Simple approach delivers all the satisfaction, without all the fuss or mess.

For each serving:
Meat from a 1½-to-2-lb lobster, cut in 1-2" chunks; leave small claws whole
1 c flour, with ½ tsp each salt & black pepper

2 large eggs, beaten w/ 4 T cornstarch & 2 T water
1 c cornmeal, with ½ - 1 tsp cayenne powder, ½ tsp garlic powder & ½ tsp onion powder
Freshly ground black or red pepper flakes

Toss lobster chunks in the seasoned flour, dip in the beaten egg mixture & roll in seasoned cornmeal. Set aside on waxed paper till all pieces are battered. Deep fry lobster, a few pieces at a time, in med-hot oil for just 30 seconds. Drain on paper toweling. Season with additional peppers to suit your taste. Serve with cool slices of melon on fresh green lettuce & some melted butter for dipping.

KISS Variation: Try **Super Simple Angry Bacon Lobster**. Cut strips of partially cooked, but still flexible, bacon in halves or thirds horizontally. Wrap each around a piece of lobster before dredging in the seasoned flour. For spiciness, try a gourmet bacon, like peppered or jalapeño. Use wooden toothpicks to hold the bacon in place, if you must. Just be sure to warn your guests! Toothpicks definitely work well if you want to use this variation for appetizers.

Veal Catarina Perfecto
This dish is naturally flavorful and light, satisfying multiple senses.

2 (4-5") veal tenderloin slices, or 4 smaller medallions
Salt & ground black pepper
Flour
2 T butter

12 thin, trimmed asparagus, grilled 3 min on med-high
2 lobster tails, halved lengthwise, plus 2 claws
½ c dry white wine

2 T lemon juice
2 thin slices Muenster or Gruyere cheese
Freshly ground black pepper

Sprinkle veal with salt & pepper; dredge in flour. Sauté in butter in skillet over med-high heat just 1 min per side. Drain on paper towels & place on 2 warmed serving dishes. Top with asparagus; keep warm. Place lobster in the same skillet for 1 min per side (2 for raw lobster). Add wine & lemon juice to deglaze pan. Turn lobster in wine mixture to coat; place 2 pieces of lobster tail on each serving of veal & asparagus. Top with cheese slice & a lobster claw. Drizzle pan juices over each, sprinkle with a bit of pepper to suit your taste. Serve immediately. Makes 2 servings.

Wen Duc Yung

I created this stir-fry dish in 1975 in honor of a college classmate who happened to be Vietnamese. I'd quipped that to me his name sounded like it should be an amazing item on a menu, so I created one.

2 cans mandarin oranges, drained, liquid set aside
2 T cornstarch
Peanut oil, coconut oil, or butter
1 large onion (sweet, if possible), sliced
1 lb fresh mushrooms, sliced
6-8 oz fresh pea pods (could use frozen)
2 T soy sauce or tamari
1 tsp ground ginger
1 box langostinos (frozen rock lobster tails)
Ground pepper
1 can sliced water chestnuts, drained
1 c canned bean sprouts (or more, as desired)
½ c chicken broth (or more)

In small bowl, mix the drained orange liquid with the cornstarch. Heat a bit of oil in wok (or very large pan) and brown the onions & mushrooms over med-high heat; push to side. Add pea pods, soy & ginger; toss and push to side. Add langostinos (and a touch more oil, if needed) & pepper; toss; push to side. Add water chestnuts, bean sprouts, broth & cornstarch-orange liquid, tossing to heat through & thicken slightly. Mix all ingredients together; toss in the mandarin oranges and serve.

KISS Tip: I also like to sprinkle sesame seeds or cashews on top.

Curried Lobster

2 cans (14-oz each) chicken broth
1 pkg (3.5-oz) curry sauce mix
1 can (14-oz) unsweetened coconut milk
½ c applesauce
2 c coconut oil
10 oz fresh spinach, washed & patted dry
Sea salt
4 raw lobster tails, without shells
2 tsp Old Bay (or other) seafood seasoning
1 T butter
1 box (5-oz) herb & butter rice, prepared
 per pkg directions

Combine broth & curry sauce mix in pan over med heat. Whisk in coconut milk & applesauce; bring to a boil. Cover & set aside. Heat coconut oil in deep pan to 350°F. Drop spinach leaves, a few at a time, into oil for just 20-30 seconds, till crispy & translucent. Remove with slotted spoon to drain on paper towels. While warm, sprinkle with sea salt. Drain off the oil; add the 1 T butter to the pan over med heat. Sauté lobster tails 5-6 min, turning occasionally. Slice crosswise into medallions. On platter or 4 serving plates, arrange lobster on warm rice; drizzle with curry sauce & garnish with crispy spinach. Makes 4 servings.

Super Simple Seafood Paella

Too many people shy away from making paella. You don't need a true paella pan. Just use any large, shallow aluminum or stainless steel skillet. You can actually enjoy it at home quite simply. Feel free to mix it up… adding or substituting squid rings, sliced Spanish chorizo or chicken pieces.

2 T olive oil
1 large onion, chopped
1 red bell pepper, chopped
1 T minced garlic
1 lb tomatoes, seeded, coarsely chopped
1 T tomato paste
1 tsp sweet paprika
1 T water mixed with ¼ tsp crumbled saffron
4 T chopped flat-leaf parsley, divided
2 lobsters (1¼ -lb each), meat removed
3 c Bomba or Arborio short-grain rice
3 (8-oz) bottles clam juice (or more, as needed)
12 mussels, scrubbed, de-bearded
12 littleneck clams, scrubbed
12 large, raw shrimp, peeled, deveined
12 sea scallops, lightly seared, if desired

Heat olive oil in large pan over med heat; sauté onion, pepper & garlic for 2-3 min. Add tomatoes; simmer 3 min. Stir in tomato paste, paprika, saffron mixture & half the parsley. (You can cover & refrigerate this sofrito sauce base overnight at this point.) Cut lobster meat in 1-2" chunks. In a very large skillet or paella pan over med heat, warm the sauce base. Add rice; stir for 1 min. Add the clam juice; bring to a boil, stirring occasionally. Reduce heat & simmer 20 min. Arrange mussels & clams on top, hinge-sides down. Arrange shrimp & scallops between them. Sprinkle with 1 c water; cover; cook 5-10 min. Distribute lobster meat over the rice (adding water or more bottled clam juice ¼ c at a time, only if paella seems dry); cover & cook 5-6 min till rice is tender. Season with salt & pepper; garnish with remaining parsley & serve directly from the pan with lemon wedges on the side.

KISS Note: We have hosted paella parties where I offer one pan of seafood paella, and a second one with a combination poultry, vegetables, and sausage. Serve with both a red and white sangria.

Lobster Florentine Crepes

¼ c butter & 1 tsp minced garlic
½ c finely chopped sweet onions
1 c thinly sliced mushrooms
¼ tsp black pepper

2 tsp fresh lemon juice
2 c fresh baby spinach leaves
1¼ c Alfredo sauce, divided
8 crepes

1 lb lobster meat chunks
¼ c chopped parsley
¼ c pine nuts or chopped macadamia nuts

Melt butter over med heat; sauté garlic, onions & mushrooms for 3 min. Add pepper, lemon juice, spinach & ¼ c of Alfredo sauce; remove from heat. Assemble crepes by dividing lobster among crepes, laying in a line thru the middle of each. Top with spinach; wrap crepes, placing seam sides-down in buttered, baking dishes, two per dish. Pour the remaining cup of Alfredo sauce over crepes. Sprinkle with nuts; bake 10 min at 350°F. Garnish with parsley & paprika. Makes 8 crepes, or 4 entrée servings.

KISS Variations: Turn this into luscious **Lobster Breakfast Crepes** by replacing Alfredo with **Hollandaise Sauce** (p. 118) & serving with poached eggs. Or present as a fancy appetizer or entrée as a 1970's flashback... **Mushroomed Lobster Popovers**. Cut hot, crispy popovers in half on each serving dish & spoon in the lobster-spinach-mushroom filling, letting it spill out between the popover halves. Serve immediately. See Popovers recipes on p. 61. An Alfredo sauce recipe is on p. 118.

Squashed Lobster Bolognese

1 c finely diced onion
½ c finely diced carrots
½ c chopped celery
1 spaghetti squash, halved

4 lobster tails, cut in large chunks, dusted with flour
4 T olive oil, divided
1 c favorite marinara sauce

1 c lobster bisque
1 T each chopped fresh parsley & thyme

Microwave onion, carrots & celery on high in ½ c water for 15 min, stirring every 5 min. Set aside. Deseed; place half a squash, cut side-down, in ½" water ; microwave on high 12 min. Repeat with other half squash. Let cool 15 min. Use a fork to rake out the squash pulp in spaghetti-like strands. Cover & keep warm. In 2 T of olive oil, stir the onion, carrot & celery combination over med heat for 5 min. Stir in marinara sauce; reduce heat to med-low; simmer 10 min. Add bisque, parsley & thyme; keep warm over low heat. In remaining 2 T olive oil, quickly sear lobster chunks over med-high heat for 2 min, turning as they caramelize. To serve, distribute spaghetti squash around the outer edges of a serving plate. Spoon sauce into center and over the squash strands. Mound lobster meat in the middle. Makes 4 servings.

Enlightened Coconut Lobster

I'd been making my Enlightened Coconut Shrimp for years, so some Super Simple lobster variation was a natural. Here's a great, easy recipe that also cuts the fat. It delivers the crispiness without frying in oil.

¾ c flour, divided
¼ tsp salt
1 pkt Stevia or Splenda sugar substitute (or 1 T sugar)
½ c skim milk (fat free)
½ c panko Japanese bread crumbs
1/3 c shredded coconut
4 lobster tails, cooked; meat from each tail sliced vertically in 2-4 strips; reserve tail shells for presentation
Coconut oil spray

Place a wire cookie cooling rack on a foil-lined baking sheet in a 400°F oven for 10 min. Meanwhile, put half the flour in a small bowl; set aside. In another bowl, combine remaining flour, salt & sugar; stir in milk; set aside. In a third bowl, combine panko & coconut. Remove heated baking sheet from oven; spray rack with coconut oil. Dredge each lobster tail strip first in flour, then in batter & then in coconut mixture. Place on the coated cookie rack. When all strips are coated, spray them with the coconut oil & bake at 400°F for 10-12 min till crispy. Serve spewing from the tail shells. With a dipping sauce.

KISS Piña Colada Sauce:
Combine ¼ c light sour cream, ¼ c liquid piña colada mix, ¼ c water-packed, canned, crushed pineapple. This sauce can be prepared ahead & refrigerated.

PASTA

Maine Lobster Lasagna

15 oz ricotta cheese	1 med onion, finely chopped	16 no-boil lasagna noodles
2 lg or ex-lg eggs	1 T minced garlic	4-6 c (2-3 lbs) cooked & diced
2 c shredded Cheddar cheese	¼ c chopped fresh parsley	lobster meat
2 c shredded mozzarella cheese	1 tsp ground black pepper	10 oz baby spinach leaves
1 c grated Parmesan cheese	2 (16-oz) jars Alfredo pasta sauce	

Stir together the ricotta, eggs, 1 c cheddar, 1 c mozzarella & ½ c Parmesan. Stir in the onion, garlic, parsley & pepper. Spread 1½ c Alfredo sauce in bottom of well-buttered 9x13" baking dish or lasagna pan. Arrange a layer of noodles on the sauce; sprinkle 1/3 of the lobster over the noodles, followed by 1/3 the ricotta cheese mixture & 1/3 of the spinach. Starting again with Alfredo sauce, repeat layering two more times. Press down with back of spoon or spatula over the whole pan to remove air spaces. Spread remaining sauce on top; sprinkle with remaining Cheddar, mozzarella & Parmesan cheeses. Cover loosely with foil; bake 35 min at 375°F. Remove foil and bake 10 min. Let stand 10 min before cutting. Makes 12 servings.

Fettuccini Seafood Fest
Fun, fast & fancy. It doesn't get better than that!

12 oz fettuccini noodles	12-oz can evaporated milk	2 c cooked shrimp
3 T butter	1 can crabmeat, drained,	½ - ¾ c shredded Parmesan
1 T minced garlic	cartilage removed	cheese
3 T flour	2 c lobster meat, cut in chunks	2 T minced fresh parsley
1 c milk	1 c chopped clams, drained	Freshly ground black pepper

Cook pasta per pkg directions. Meanwhile, in large pan, melt butter; sauté garlic 2 min. Whisk in flour till blended. Remove from heat; stirring while gradually adding the milks. Return to heat and bring to boil over med heat, stirring till thickened. Add the seafood & half the cheese. Drain pasta & serve topped with seafood mixture, sprinkled with remaining Parmesan, parsley & pepper. Makes 6 servings.

KISS Tip: You can Super Simplify this by replacing the butter, garlic, flour, milk, evaporated milk, and half the cheese with a jar of your favorite Alfredo pasta sauce.

Spicy Lobster Linguine

1 c dry white wine (or vodka)
1 c salted water
4 live lobsters (1½ lbs each)
Coarse sea salt & ground pepper
1 lb linguine pasta
3 T olive oil
1 T finely minced garlic
Crushed red pepper flakes
3 c drained, coarsely chopped canned tomatoes
2 T chopped fresh flat-leaf parsley

Bring wine & the 1 c water to boil in large pot. Add lobsters; steam 10-12 min. Remove & let cool at room temp. Remove tail, claw & knuckle meat. Halve tail meat lengthwise & then crosswise; set aside. Boil salted water; cook linguine al dente, per pkg directions. Heat olive oil over med heat in a lg pan; sauté garlic for 2 min. Then stir in red pepper flakes, tomatoes & parsley. Simmer 2 min, seasoning with salt & pepper, if you desire. To serve, spoon sauce over the hot pasta. Arrange lobster meat chunks on top; serve immediately to 4 smiling diners! Offer freshly grated parmesan cheese on the side.

Cannelloni Cape Elizabeth

Cape Elizabeth lies on the coast of Maine just below Portland. We love the rocky coastline, the lighthouse, and the lobster! This recipe honors this iconic spot in Maine.

1 T chopped thyme or rosemary
8 T softened butter, divided
Salt & pepper, to suit your taste
2 lobster tails, halved lengthwise & 4 claws
1 lg sweet onion, finely chopped
½ - ¾ lb sliced mushrooms
8-12 oz baby spinach leaves
½ c mascarpone cheese
1 c lobster meat in ½" pieces
4 fresh pasta sheets (5x5" each), blanched
½ c dry white wine
1 c vegetable or seafood broth
1½ c heavy cream
½ c shredded parmesan cheese
4 sprigs fresh thyme

Mix thyme, half the butter, salt & pepper. Place lobster tails (shell sides down, if using shells) & claw meat in buttered, baking dish; spread herbed butter on each piece; set aside. In lg skillet over med-high heat, melt remaining 4 T butter; sauté half the onions & all mushrooms 4-5 min. Season with salt & pepper. Stir in spinach, cover & reduce heat to med-low for 1 min, just to wilt the spinach. Remove from heat, uncover; cool 10 min. Stir in mascarpone & diced lobster meat. Divide among the 4 pieces of pasta; roll into tubes. Place stuffed tubes, seam-sides-down in baking pan with large lobster pieces. Bake 10 min at 325°F. Place remaining onions in wine in pan over med-high heat; bring to boil. Let boil till liquid is reduced by half. Stir in broth; boil till reduced by half again. Stir in heavy cream; season with salt & pepper. Reduce liquid to half. Place one cannelloni on each of 4 warmed serving plates with half a lobster tail & one claw. Divide cream sauce over them. Sprinkle with parmesan & garnish with thyme.

KISS Tips: To fill blanched manicotti tubes, squeeze lobster filling in with pastry bag or from a heavy-duty plastic bag with one corner snipped off.

Super Simple Lobster Fra Diavolo

4 T olive oil
4 T butter
1 tsp minced garlic
1 large onion, chopped
28 oz canned crushed or diced tomatoes in sauce

1 hot pepper, seeded & halved
½ tsp crushed red pepper flakes
1 tsp dried, crushed thyme
½ c chopped fresh parsley
1 tsp dried basil
1 tsp dried oregano

1 c wine (white or red)
Salt & pepper, to suit your taste
2 c lg pieces lobster meat (claws halved, tails in medallion slices)
Hot pasta

Melt butter in olive oil in large skillet or pot; sauté garlic & onion over med heat 2-3 min. Stir in tomatoes. Add remaining ingredients, except for lobster. Cover, reduce heat to low, & simmer 20 min. Remove hot pepper halves. Stir in lobster. Simmer 2-3 min; turn off heat & let sit (still covered for 3-4 min. Toss some of the sauce with your choice of pasta (penne, linguine, etc). Spoon the lobster pieces on top. Serve immediately with grated parmesan or Romano cheese & the extra sauce on the side as gravy. Makes 2 generous servings.

KISS Note: This needs nothing more than a side salad and some hot crusty garlic bread.

KISS Variation: Make this **Seafood Fra Diavolo** by using a variety of seafood. Try adding 4 shelled jumbo shrimp, 4 sea scallops, 6 little neck clams (in their shells), and 8 mussels (in their shells) at the same time as the lobster. Or skip the pasta, double the sauce and go for **Sassy Short Cut Bouillabaisse**. Divide the seafood among bowls and pour the sauce over it. Serve with toasted garlic or cheesy garlic bread slices sticking out of the soup. (Into the sauce, stir in a bit of seafood or vegetable broth & clam juice, if you prefer a thinner consistency for your soup.)

STUFFED & COMBOS

Half lobster stuffed with **Super Simple Lobster Amazing**

Lazy Lobster Stuffed Filet Mignon

24-oz beef tenderloin with large pocket cut perpendicularly to within ½" of bottom on 1 side
2 lg lobster tails, halved lengthwise & cut in small chunks
2 T melted butter
1 T lemon juice
4 thick slices bacon, partially cooked, but still flexible
1 c butter
1 c sliced green onions (white & green portions)
1 c dry white wine
1/8 tsp garlic salt

Lay tenderloin in shallow roasting pan, with pocket opening facing up. Stuff lobster chunks into the 4 filet pockets. Combine melted butter & lemon juice; drizzle into the pockets over the lobster. Close pockets by wrapping a slice of bacon over each one, fastening with wooden toothpicks, if needed. Bake at 350°F for 10-12 min for rare, 12-14 min for medium rare, or 24-26 min for medium. Meanwhile, melt the 1 c butter in saucepan over med heat; stir in green onion, wine & garlic salt. Cook just 30-60 seconds. Slice the tenderloin into filets, cutting across the pocket. Place each stuffed filet on a serving plate with potato & a vegetable. Spoon the warm sauce over each filet. Serve hot.

KISS Tip: This is delicious served with garlic mashed potato and a green vegetable of your choice.

Lobster Double-Stuffed Lobster

This recipe was inspired by my jaw-dropping experience near Jamaica's Rose Hall in the mid-1970's. I'd never before even heard of stuffing a lobster with the meat of another lobster. Here's our Super Simple take on getting it done… juicy and sweet.

For each serving:
1 lobster (1½ to 2 lbs), freshly steamed
4-6 T butter
2 T Worcestershire sauce
1/8 c minced celery
1/8 c minced sweet onion
½ to ¾ c crushed buttery crackers (such as Ritz)
¼ tsp lemon pepper
1/8 tsp garlic powder or garlic salt
2 T freshly grated or shredded parmesan cheese
½ - ¾ c additional chunks of cooked lobster meat (tails, knuckles & claws)
Paprika

Twist off lobster tail; remove tail meat, taking care to keep the back of the tail shell in one basic piece, as you will be putting the lobster & stuffing back into it for serving. (Do this by cutting down the underside of the tail with kitchen scissors.) Crack claws & place the lobster body on its back on a warmed serving platter; use kitchen scissors to cut up the center between the legs. Place the tail on the platter, recreating the look of a whole lobster. Cut tail meat into large medallion slices; put them back into the empty tail shell. In large skillet, melt butter; sauté celery & onion 3 min over med heat. Stir in all remaining ingredients, except for the paprika. Mound the lobster stuffing over the tail meat and onto the body between the small legs. Sprinkle with paprika; bake 10 min at 400°F. Serve hot with more melted butter for dipping.

KISS Tip: For even more seafood flavor, add a cup of crabmeat to the stuffing. For some island zip, add 1-2 T hot sauce along with the Worcestershire.

Chicken and Lobster Francaîse
In the mid-1980's I recall getting my first taste of Chicken Francaise. Then came the same treatment for veal and then shrimp. I just love the light crispness of the edges of the batter and the zip of the buttery, tart wine sauce. This makes a perfect surf and turf.

Meat of 2-3 large lobster tails, sliced in medallions
1 boneless chicken breast, halved & lightly pounded (or boneless thighs, as you prefer)
Flour
3 eggs, beaten
¼ c grated Romano cheese
½ tsp salt
Freshly ground black pepper, to suit your taste
½ c coconut or olive oil
2 T butter
¼ c fresh (or frozen) lemon juice
½ c white wine
2-4 thin round slices of lemon
2 T chopped fresh parsley

Dredge lobster medallions & chicken cutlets in flour; set on waxed paper. In a bowl, beat the egg, cheese, salt & pepper together. Dip protein pieces in egg batter; cook them in (350°F) hot oil, over med-high heat in a large skillet. (Cook chicken 2 min per side & lobster 1 min per side.) Remove with slotted spoon to drain on wire rack over paper towels. Pour out remaining oil. Add 2 T butter to the same skillet; reduce heat to med. Stir in lemon juice, wine, a bit more black pepper & the lemon slices. Cook 2-3 min until wine liquid reduces by about half; stir in the fresh parsley. Place a chicken cutlet & half the lobster on each of two plates. Top with lemon slices & pour the lemon-wine sauce over each of the two servings.

💋**KISS Tip**: This is scrumptious served with a green vegetable & some fettucine or penne. Serve the pasta with a red sauce, or make double or triple the lemon-wine sauce & use the same sauce for the pasta as on the chicken & lobster.

Grilled Lamb Chops and Lobster

4 lamb chops (1½" thick)
Olive oil
Coarse sea salt & ground black pepper
½ c butter
1 tomato, seeded & chopped
Leaves from 3 sprigs fresh thyme
2 large lobster tails (in shells), with the underbelly softer shell cut out with kitchen scissors
½ lb pea pods, steamed crisp; tossed with butter

Brush lamb chops with olive oil; season with salt & pepper. Grill on preheated grate over med-high heat 4 min per side for med-rare (6 min per side for med). Let rest under a light tent of foil for 5 min before serving. Melt butter in small pan over low heat; stir in tomato, thyme, salt & pepper; cook 5 min. Keep warm. Brush shell & belly sides of lobster tails with olive oil; season with salt & pepper. Grill shell-side-down on med-high heat for 2-3 min (5 min if using raw lobster); turn over. Spoon some tomato butter onto exposed tail meat; cook 2-3 min (5 if using raw lobster). Plate 2 lamb chops & 1 lobster tail with half the pea pods; spoon tomato butter over the lobster. Makes 2 servings.

**KISS Tip**: If you like fresh mint, garnish your lamb chops with fresh mint leaves.

Sides & Veggies

Baconed Lobster Succotash
Though the recipe has been modified in the KISS kitchens, the inspiration came from the chef and owner of a long-gone (& greatly missed) Windham, New Hampshire restaurant, called Loafers. They served their crab version alongside a seared salmon. We'd order the salmon just to get the succotash!

8-10 slices apple-smoked bacon, diced	2 c frozen baby lima beans or 1" cuts of thin asparagus stalks	2 c (1 lb) coarsely chopped lobster meat
1 c finely chopped sweet onion	3 c heavy cream	Kosher or sea salt & freshly ground pepper
3 c fresh or frozen corn kernels	¼ c finely sliced green onions (green portions)	

Put half the corn in a pan with the cream; simmer over med-low heat, stirring occasionally, till reduced & slightly thickened. In a large skillet, cook bacon over med heat until crisp. Add onions; sauté 2-3 min in the bacon fat. Add lima beans or asparagus; simmer 2-3 more min. Stir in remaining corn & the green onions, followed by the cream reduction, lobster & seasonings. Makes 4 decadent servings.

Savory Lobster Stuffing

Per serving:	¼ c chopped onion, cooked	Dash hot sauce, such as Frank's Red Hot
6-8 oz cooked lobster meat, coarsely chopped	2 T chopped celery	1 T sherry
¼ tsp. ground black pepper	12-14 crumbled Ritz crackers	½ c butter, melted
2 T lobster tamalley	¼ tsp garlic salt	
	¼ c shredded parmesan cheese	

Combine, mixing well & serve, warmed or at room temperature.

💋**KISS Notes:** This makes a great side dish. Or mound it atop a lobster before baking. Serve it stuffed into 2-3" slices of celery stalks as tapas. Spoon it into mushroom caps or mini phyllo pastry cups & quickly bake as hot appetizers. Mound on pork chops, beef, or chicken entrees for a surf & turf touch. Serve in a fresh croissant as a sandwich. Spoon it inside an omelet or top it with a poached or fried egg for breakfast.

💋**KISS Variation:** Make this a **Lovely Lobster Melt** for a decadent open-faced sandwich. Eliminate the cracker crumbs. Mound the stuffing on 2 toasted English muffin halves and sprinkle with shredded Gruyere or Monterey Jack cheese before baking or broiling.

Simply Out-of-This-World Lobster Mac-and-Cheese

I see menus with options for a little lobster, more lobster, or a lot of lobster in their macaroni and cheese. Helloooo! If I'm ordering lobster macaroni and cheese, hit me with a decent portion of lobster, please! Our KISS kitchen believes neither you nor your guests should have to search through pasta to find the lobster, even in a side dish.

2 lbs penne, curly, or corkscrew pasta, cooked in salted water per pkg directions to al dente; drained
3-4 T olive oil
3 oz cream cheese, cut in bits
2 c shredded Gruyere cheese
1 c freshly grated or shaved Parmesan cheese
2 c grated Cheddar or mild provolone cheese
3 c heavy cream
1 T truffle oil (yes, the flavor is worth it)
Coarse sea salt & freshly ground black pepper (to suit your taste)
4-6 c cooked lobster meat chunks, with tails sliced into ½" medallions
1 lb fresh baby spinach leaves, (coarsely chopped, if desired)

In a large bowl, drizzle oil over cooked pasta; toss well to distribute. Stir in cream cheese and Gruyere till smooth. Then stir in remaining cheeses, cream, truffle oil & seasonings, followed by lobster meat, and spinach. Transfer to large baking dish; bake at 425°F for 20-25 min, just till bubbly & hot. Serves 6-8.

KISS Tips:
- Keep lobster claw meat intact to use as garnishes, rather than stirring into the pasta.
- If steaming lobsters yourself, just boil 2-3" of water to which you have added up to ¼ c sea salt. Steam lobsters 12-15 min with 2 halved lemons. (Squeeze juice & drop in the rinds, too.) You need no herbs or spices, but if you want, try a little fresh thyme or parsley.

KISS Notes: Try adding ½ - 1 cup crumbled, cooked bacon! Take this to another level of buttery marvelousness by topping the baking dish with a tube of crushed Ritz crackers tossed with 6-8 T melted butter. The topping bakes to a golden crispness that compliments the smooth sweetness of the lobster & pasta. If you don't have truffle oil, try substituting 1 T sherry. Though not the same, it is tasty. For **Lobacious Mac & Cheese Fritters**, omit spinach. Chill the cooked mac & cheese. Scoop with a spoon; use your hands to form 1 – 1½" balls. Roll in panko bread crumbs and brown in butter, deep fry for 3-5 min at 350°F, or spray with coconut or olive oil and bake at 375°F for 10-12 min, turning once. Serve these decadent delights with warmed marinara sauce for dipping. The fritters also make a wonderfully satisfying side dish with a toasty bowl of your favorite tomato soup!

Shitake Lobster Risotto

4 T extra virgin olive oil
1 c chopped sweet onion
¼ c finely chopped red onion
1-2 tsp minced garlic
2 c steamed & ¼"-sliced Shitake mushrooms
2 c Arborio rice
5 c hot chicken broth
1 tsp white pepper
2 tsp finely snipped chives
¼ c grated Parmesan cheese
1 T butter
2½ c lobster meat, cut in ½" pieces

Heat olive oil in sauce pan over med heat; sauté onions & garlic 2 min. Add mushrooms; sauté 3 min. Add rice; sauté 1 min. Add 1 c of chicken broth; lower heat & simmer, stirring often, till liquid is absorbed. Add remaining chicken broth, 1 cup at a time, till rice is cooked & creamy. Stir in pepper, chives, Parmesan & butter. Then gently fold in lobster.

💋**KISS Variation:** Turn this into **Jacked Up Risotto** by adding 1 c fresh lightly steamed corn kernels & stirring in ½ c shredded Monterey Jack cheese at the end. Or just go cheesy & eliminate the veggies. Topping with a whole lobster tail & a sprinkle of chives or parsley adds pure lobaciousness!

Baked Lobster Broccoli
This beauty could even convert the most dedicated anti-broccoli fanatic.

8 oz cream cheese (plain, chive or garden vegetable), softened to room temp
3 T softened butter
¼ c milk
1/8 – ¼ tsp garlic powder

20 oz frozen broccoli florets or chopped broccoli, cooked al dente, drained
2 c bite-sized, cooked lobster pieces (fresh or frozen, thawed) (about 1 lb)

½ c crumbled Ritz (or other buttery) crackers
¼ c grated Parmesan cheese
¼ c shredded Cheddar cheese
2 T melted butter
Paprika

In a bowl, blend cream cheese, butter, milk & garlic powder together. Stir in hot broccoli & lobster. Spoon into 6 well-buttered ramekins, large custard cups, or small individual baking dishes. In a bowl, combine cracker crumbs, cheese & melted butter. Sprinkle over tops of the 6 dishes. Add a dash of paprika. Bake at 400°F for 10 min, just to heat the lobster & melt the cheese. Makes 6 servings.

Lobster Cauliflower au Gratin
After being served a cheesy lobster cauliflower side dish once in a restaurant some decades ago, I went searching for a recipe online. They're out there with 20+ ingredients and multiple steps and fanci-tudes. We gave it the ol' Super Simple treatment and absolutely LOVED the results!

¾ c heavy cream
¾ c mascarpone cheese (or plain cream cheese)
½ c white wine
2 tsp white truffle oil

½ tsp crushed dried thyme
1-lb bag frozen cauliflower florets, cooked 3 min, drained
2 c bite-sized pieces of cooked lobster (1 lb)

1 c panko (Japanese) bread crumbs (or Ritz crackers)
¼ c grated Parmesan cheese
3 T melted butter

In a bowl, whisk cream, cheese, wine, truffle oil & thyme together well. Add hot cauliflower & lobster; stir well & season with salt & pepper, to suit your taste. Pour into 1 large or 6 individual, well-buttered baking dishes; bake at 350°F for 10 min. Remove from oven; raise heat to 400°F. In a bowl, combine crumbs, Parmesan cheese & melted butter; sprinkle over lobster cauliflower gratin. Return to oven; bake 5-10 min at the higher temperature till browned & bubbly. Serve hot. Makes 6 servings.

KISS Tip: To "fancify," think "Veal Oscar." Spoon hot cauliflower gratin in the center of each serving plate, top with thin, grilled spears of asparagus & a lobster tail or half on top.

Lobster Mashed Potatoes

1 lg onion, diced
2 stalks celery, diced
2 carrots, peeled & diced
1 T peppercorns
1 tsp dried thyme
2-lb live lobster
½ c butter
¼ c flour
2-3 T tomato paste
¼ c sherry
1 qt heavy whipping cream
Salt & ground black pepper
4 large portions of your favorite mashed potatoes

Make lobster stock in large pot by bringing 2 qts water to a boil with the onion, celery, carrots, peppercorns & thyme. Add the lobster & boil 8 min. Remove lobster from pot. Remove tail, claws & knuckles. Return body to the pot. Remove meat from tail, claws & knuckles; cut in ½" chunks & set aside. Return shells to the pot. Boil another 10-20 min. Strain to remove the solids, which can be discarded. Melt the butter in the pot over med-low heat. Remove from heat & whisk in flour till smooth. Gradually stir in just ½ c of the lobster stock till smooth, followed by the tomato paste & sherry. Raise heat to med, & let reduce by half. Gradually stir in the cream. Just before serving time, stir in half the lobster meat; season with salt & pepper to suit your taste. Fold remaining lobster meat into hot mashed potatoes; mound on 4 dinner plates beside green vegetable, such as asparagus, and a pan-seared salmon filet or other seafood entrée, such as sea scallops. Divide lobster sauce among the plates, smothering the potatoes and over part of the entrée. Garnish with fresh parsley or sliced green onions & a lemon wedge.

KISS Notes: Try adding small, fresh, sweet peas at the end. Oh, yes! This is also great substituting seasoned, mashed or riced cauliflower for the spuds, creating **Lobster Mashed Cauliflower**. Also try adding some sautéed mushroom slices. You can even use these to stuff twice-baked potatoes or even a lobster itself. Make **Double Lobster Shepherd's Pie** by microwaving ½ c diced baby carrots, 1 c chopped sweet onion & 1 c sliced mushrooms, & 2 T butter on high for 2 min. Transfer to buttered 9x9" baking dish. Sprinkle with 1 c fresh or frozen corn kernels & 2 c lobster chunks. Pour the above lobster sauce over the top. Then spread with the lobster mashed potatoes. Sprinkle with ¼ - ½ c shredded Parmesan cheese. Bake at 400°F for 30 min. Sprinkle with chopped fresh chives or parsley & serve hot.

Twice-Baked Lobster Potatoes

Photo courtesy of Steven Raichen

2 live Maine lobsters (1½ lbs each)
4 lg baking potatoes, baked
8 T butter
Fine sea salt & freshly ground black pepper
4 T butter
1/3 c onion, finely chopped
½ c mushrooms, finely chopped
1 c dry white vermouth
½ c **Crème Fraîche** (recipe follows)
½ c grated Jarlsburg, Swiss or Cheddar cheese
1 to 2 T Heavy Cream
2 T grated Parmesan cheese
Diagonally sliced green onions, for garnish

Steam or boil lobsters for a total of 8 min. Let cool a bit; clean out all the meat from tail, claws, knuckles & body. Slice top of potatoes & scrape out all potato pulp into a bowl, taking care not to puncture the skins. Mash the potato with 8 T butter; set aside. Season the insides of the potato shells with salt & pepper. In skillet, melt the 4 T butter; sauté chopped onion & mushrooms for 5-6 min. Add vermouth; raise heat & boil, stirring often till liquid has all but boiled away. Stir in the lobster; season with salt & pepper to suit your taste. Then stir in the **Crème Fraîche** & remove from heat. Stir in the mashed potatoes, Jarlsberg cheese & heavy cream. Spoon mixture into potato skin shells, mounding on top. Sprinkle tops with Parmesan cheese. Bake 15 min at 400°F; garnish with onions. Makes 4.

Crème Fraîche

1 c heavy or whipping cream
1 c sour cream

Whisk heavy & sour creams together. Let stand at room temp till thickened. Cover & refrigerate at least 4 hours. Makes 2 cups.

Lobster Veggie Sizzling Stir-Fry
Have fun with this by using your favorite veggies or add additional seafood, such as scallops & shrimp.

2 T peanut, coconut, or olive oil
1 sweet onion, halved & thinly sliced
2 c peeled, sliced yellow summer squash
½ c thinly sliced button mushrooms
2 c angle-sliced fresh asparagus cuts
½ c julienned sweet red peppers

½ c tamari or low-sodium soy
Freshly ground black pepper
1 T minced ginger
¼ c thinly sliced green onions
1c sliced lobster meat
Brown rice, hot
2 T sesame seeds

Heat oil over med heat in nonstick wok. Stir-fry onion 2 min; add squash; stir 2-3 min. Add mushrooms, asparagus, peppers & 2 T water; stir 3-4 min more. Stir in tamari, black pepper, ginger, green onions, and lobster meat; cook 1 min. Serve over hot rice, sprinkled with sesame seeds. Makes 4 servings.

KISS Tip: Turn this into an entrée by increasing the amount of lobster to 2-3 cups.

Photo courtesy of Henry Perks

Sauces & Condiments

Lobster Butter
Use lobster butter to add another layer of decadence to dipping your steamed lobster meat. Or try it for any other fish by itself or in a cream sauce.

Leftover shells & legs from 1 large lobster (that you just gleefully devoured)
½ c butter
2 T water

Melt butter in sauté pan over med-low heat; add shells & water. Let simmer 10 min, but don't let the butter boil. Remove shells; pour lobster butter into a small container. Refrigerate. Skim off butter when it hardens. Makes about ½ c.

KISS Tip: Substitute shrimp shells to create **Shrimp Butter**.

Super Simple Lobster Pesto Sauce

1 T butter
3 T basil pesto sauce (supermarket or homemade)
¼ c white wine
1/8 c bottled clam juice
1½ c cooked, diced lobster meat
3 T grated parmesan cheese
Salt & pepper, to suit your taste
Chopped fresh parsley

Melt butter in sauté pan over med-low heat; stir in pesto. Stir in wine & clam juice; let simmer 3-4 min. Stir in lobster, cheese & seasonings. Serve over your choice of hot pasta, garnished with fresh parsley. Makes 2 servings.

Lobster Mango Salsa

This is amazing at an Acapulco-themed party. As with most salsa, versatility is only limited by your imagination!

3 c (1½ lb) lobster meat, cut in bite-size chunks
3 small fresh mangos, peeled, pitted & diced
1/3 - ½ c red onion, finely chopped
2/3 c sweet red bell pepper, finely chopped
2 T chopped fresh cilantro
3 T fresh lime juice
3/4 tsp grated lime peel
1/8 tsp each coarse sea salt & ground black pepper

Toss all ingredients together in a large bowl. Cover & refrigerate up to 3 hours. Makes about 5 cups.

KISS Note: For some kick, add 1/8 tsp ground cayenne pepper with your seasonings.

KISS Tips: Have fun with serving ideas.
- Try this as a surf salad on a crisp lettuce leaf beside your grilled steak.
- Spoon it onto lettuce leaves in pita pockets for a simple, tangy sandwich.
- Stir it into pasta salad for a splendidly fresh taste.
- Mound it atop crispy baguette slices, with or without a bit of cheese spread.

Photo courtesy of David diVeroli

Alfredo Sauce
There are plenty of good bottled sauces, but here's a Super Simple one you can make.

1½ sticks (¾ c) butter (no substitutes)
1½ c heavy or whipping cream
1¾ c freshly grated Parmesan cheese
Freshly ground black pepper, to suit your taste

Melt butter over med heat in a saucepan. Whisk in the cream till simmering. Stir in cheese until melted. Use as needed for a recipe or toss with fresh, hot fettucine pasta. Serve with a fresh grind of pepper on top.

KISS Notes: Depending upon your use for the sauce, this is wonderful with broken pieces of crisply cooked bacon, sautéed chopped onion or sliced mushrooms, and chunks of lobster meat. With seafood dishes, try adding ½ c bottled clam juice. Add large chunks of lobster meat and plenty of canned or fresh littleneck clams and serve over hot linguine for a **Super Simple Clobster Sauce**. With clams, I also like to add a dash or more of a hot sauce, such as Frank's Red Hot. With a garnish of fresh parsley, you are ready to serve.

Hollandaise Sauce
This is great for a Lobster Benedict, Lobster Crepes, or any other lobster dish that calls for a lemony butter sauce, or on a cooked vegetable, such as asparagus or broccoli. Use a simple package mix, or try this Super Simple recipe that I've been using since the mid-1970's.

3 egg yolks
2 T lemon juice
½ tsp prepared yellow mustard
Dash cayenne pepper
½ c butter

Place egg yolks, lemon juice, mustard & cayenne in blender. Blend on low speed just till mixed. Melt butter in saucepan till bubbly, but not brown. Cover blender; turn on low speed; slowly pour about a third of the hot butter in a thin stream into blender. Turn blender to high speed; slowly pour in remaining butter, blending till smooth & thickened. Makes about 1 cup.

Your Just Desserts

Melt-in-Your-Mouth Lobster Strudel

½ c chopped sweet onion
3 T butter
1 c dry vermouth
4 lg egg yolks, beaten
¼ c snipped parsley
1 tsp salt
½ tsp ground white pepper
4 oz cream cheese, cubed
2 to 2½ c lobster meat, cut in ½ to ¾" pieces
8 phyllo dough sheets, thawed
½ c melted butter
½ c fine bread crumbs

Sauté onions in butter over med heat till golden; stir in vermouth; boil till reduced to 1/3 cup. In a small bowl, whisk a spoonful of butter mixture into beaten egg yolks. Then slowly stir egg yolks into butter & onion mixture. Add parsley, salt & pepper, then cream cheese, stirring till cheese is melted. Gently fold in lobster. Place 1 sheet phyllo on cookie sheet; brush with butter; sprinkle with 1 T bread crumbs. Add a second sheet, butter & crumbs. Repeat 2 more times for a total of 4 phyllo sheets in the stack. Mound half the lobster mixture lengthwise on the phyllo stack, leaving a 1" pastry border. Roll phyllo into 2" thick roll. Repeat process to make a second roll. Brush tops of the rolls with remaining melted butter. With serrated knife, make partial slices (no more than ½" deep) in roll before baking or freezing. Bake 15 min at 350°F. Without opening oven door, increase temp to 450°F for 5 - 10 min. Remove from oven; let rest at room temp for 10 min. To serve, cut in slices at the points where you made the partial cuts. Makes 2 strudels.

KISS Note: This is a wonderful appetizer or luncheon entrée. But as dessert, it brings new decadence to your dining. Garnish a warm or room temperature dessert slice with some fresh whipped cream and let it all melt in your mouth! If serving as an appetizer or entrée, sprinkle slices with some extra chopped fresh parsley. (Or sprinkle parsley atop the whipped cream dollop.)

Cha-Cha-Chocolate Lobster
If you love lobster and you love chocolate, well… get ready to double your passion power in one straight over-the-top dessert treat!

4 oz semi-sweet chocolate, chopped
½ c milk
½ - 1 tsp pure vanilla extract

1 T butter
Meat from 1 freshly steamed 1½ lb lobster

Combine chocolate, milk, vanilla & butter in a microwave-safe bowl. Microwave on high, stirring every 15 seconds, just until smooth. Dip warm lobster chunks in the chocolate & savor the flavor! Makes 2 servings.

KISS Tip: Just one thing adds to the decadence of this dessert: Savor the lobster while sipping on chilled champagne!

Cool Coast Cheesecake

16 oz cream cheese, softened at room temp
8 oz mascarpone cheese, at room temp
3 lg or ex-lg eggs
1/3 c sugar

½ tsp pure vanilla extract
¾ c all-purpose flour
1½ c cooked lobster pieces, cut in ½" pieces
½ c cooked shrimp, diced

½ c chopped sweet onion
¼ c thinly sliced green onions
¼ tsp ground nutmeg
½ tsp salt
¼ tsp ground white pepper

Line a 6" diameter cheesecake or spring form pan (with 3" sides) with parchment paper. With an electric mixer on med-hi speed, beat cream cheese & mascarpone for 3 min. Add eggs, one at a time, beating after each egg. Mix in sugar & vanilla, followed by flour. Using a rubber spatula, gently fold in the lobster, shrimp, onion, green onion, nutmeg, salt & white pepper. Pour into the prepared pan; bake at 325°F for 45-50 min till top is golden & center is almost firm. Cool; then cover top with plastic wrap; refrigerate at least 6 hrs before serving. To serve, top each slice with a dollop of whipped cream.

KISS Notes: Try this as a brunch or luncheon entrée. Simply eliminate the sugar, vanilla extract & nutmeg; add 2 tsp minced garlic. You could also use it as an appetizer spread and serve it with crackers or fresh, crunchy vegetables.

Peared Lobster Peaches

1 c diced lobster meat
½ c diced pears (fresh or canned)
2 T mayonnaise
1 packet Splenda sweetener (or 2 tsp sugar)
¼ tsp salt
1/8 tsp freshly ground pepper
¼ c orange juice (mixed w mango, if you can find it)
6 large, ripe peach halves (or canned, if you must)
Whipped cream, for garnish

Combine lobster, pears, mayonnaise, sweetener, salt, pepper & orange juice. Stuff the peaches with the mixture; chill at least 1 hour. Serve with a dollop of whipped cream. Makes 6 servings.

KISS Tip: Eliminate sweetener & whipped cream garnish to serve as a "fancified" side dish with poultry, steak or tuna.

KISS Variation: Using only fresh peach halves, try turning these gems into **Grilled Stuffed Peaches**. Cook the cut side of the peaches on an oil-sprayed med-hot grill for 1 min. Turn them over, stuff, close grill cover, and cook 3 min. This works with either side dish or dessert combinations.

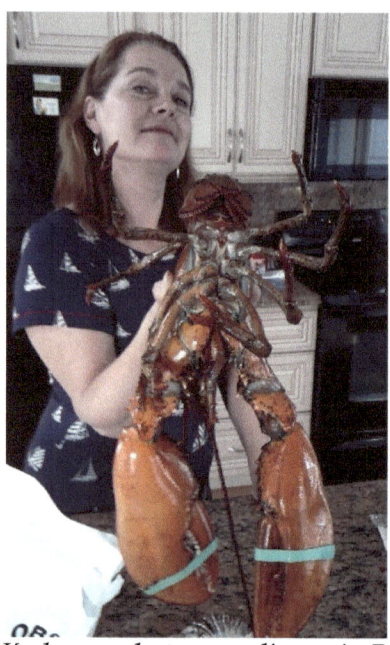
Our friend, Pat McKerley, ready to prep dinner in Rye, New Hampshire

*2008 Author's family enjoying lobster backyard picnic.
From left to right: nephew Tom Burnham, brother Jim Burnham, father Robert Burnham, sister Deborah Burnham, and mother Glenna Burnham*

Where to Buy Lobster

Most supermarkets sell live and cooked lobsters. However, if you are fortunate to have access to a true lobster pound, this is even better, as you frequently are buying fresh lobsters they actually caught. Many of these lobster pounds are adept at shipping live, cooked, and/or frozen lobsters and tails. Some ship lobster meat, all removed from the shells for you. Here are just a few. Call or check their websites.

We provide a longer list and more detailed information on the **GoodLiving123.com** blog website. Additional markets and pounds can be found with the "Where to Indulge in Lobster" section, as many lobster and fish markets also offer dine in and take out options.

🫦MAINE

Calendar Island Maine Lobster	Portland	CalendarSeafood.com
Cape Porpoise Lobster Company	Kennebunkport	CapePorpoiseLobster.com
Captain Hook's Fish Market	Wells	CaptainHooksTakeOut.com
Chrissy D. Lobster Company	Kittery	ChrissyDLobster.com
Get Maine Lobster	(web only)	GetMaineLobster.com
Lobster Anywhere	Penobscott Bay	LobsterAnywhere.com
Joe Lane Lobsterman	Damariscotta	(no website)
Lunt's Gateway Lobster Pound	Trenton	LuntsGatewayLobster.com
Maine Lobster Direct	Portland	MaineLobsterDirect.com
Maine Lobster Now	South Portland	MaineLobsterNow.com
Maine Lobster Outlet	York	MaineLobsterOutlet.com
Off the Boat Lobsters	York	OffTheBoatLobsters.com
Pemaquid Lobster Co-op	Pemaquid	PemaquidLobsterCo-Op.com
Pine Point Fisherman's Co-op	Scarborough	LobsterCo-Op.com
Sea Salt Lobster	Saco	SeaSaltLobsterRestaurant.com
Southern Maine Lobster Company	York	Facebook.com/Southern-Maine-Lobster-Co
Taylor Lobster Company	Kittery	TaylorLobster.com
Young's Lobster Pound	Belfast	YoungsLobsterPound.webs.com

NEW HAMPSHIRE

Al's Seafood	North Hampton	AlsSeafoodNH.com
Captain Don's Lobster Pound	Seabrook	CaptDons.com
Defiant Lobster Company	Hampton	DefiantLobster.com
Donahue's Fish Market	Plaistow	DonahuesFishMarket.com
Lobster Claw II	Derry	LobsterClaw2.com
Lobster Connection	Tilton	(no website)
Makris Lobster & Steak	Concord	EatALobster.com
Northland Lobster Co.	Conway	Facebook.com/Northland-Lobster-Company
Petey's Summertime Seafood	Rye	Peteys.com
Rye Harbor Lobster Pound	Rye Harbor	Facebook.com/RyeHarborLobsterPound.com
Sander's Lobster Company	Portsmouth	SandersLobster.com
Shyer's Lobster Pound	Salem	ShyersLobsters.com
Smitty's State Pier Lobster Pound	Hampton	SmittysLobster.com
Yankee Fisherman's Co-op	Seabrook	YankeeFish.com

OTHER

167 Raw	Nantucket	167Raw.com
Atlantic Seafood Market	Old Saybrook, CT	AtlanticSeafoodMarket.com
Best Seafood Place	Orlando, FL	BestSeafoodPlaceFL.com
Champlin's Seafood	Narragansett, RI	Champlins.com
David's Fish Market	Salisbury, MA	DavidsFishMarket.com
Doug's Seafood	Bonita Springs, FL	DougsSeafood.com
Ed's Lobster Bar	Manhattan, NY	LobsterBarNYC.com
Green Harbor Lobster Pound	Green Harbor, MA	Facebook.com/Green-Harbor-Lobster-Pound
Guilford Lobster Pound	Guilford, CT	GuilfordLobsterPound.com
James Hook & Co.	Boston, MA	JamesHookLobster.com
Jordan Lobster Farms	Island Park, NY	JordanLobsterFarms.com
The Lobster Guy	Narragansett, RI	TheLobsterGuy.com
Narragansett Bay Lobsters	Narragansett, RI	NarragansettBayLobsters.com
Orleans Lobster Pound	Orleans, MA	OrleansLobsterPound.com
Red Hook Lobster Pound	(several), NY & DC	RedHookLobster.com
Red's Best at Boston Public Market	Boston, MA	RedsBest.com
Rowayton Seafood	Rowayton, CT	RowaytonSeafood.com
Yankee Lobster Co.	Boston, MA	YankeeLobsterCompany.com

Where to Indulge in Lobster

Many times we want to know where we can sit down to a succulent steamed lobster with warm, melted butter… or get a perfect lobster roll… or enjoy a steamy bowl of lobster stew or bisque… or scarf down some other mouth-watering, lobster-laden dish. Naturally, there are far more restaurants in the Northeastern USA alone than I could possibly list, but here are more than just a few to get you started. I focused on spots that offer at least a lobster roll, if not whole lobsters, with my apologies to any favorite spots of yours that I have missed. A more complete list is available on the **GoodLiving123.com** blog.

The blog also includes phone numbers, awards, and the types of lobster items on their menus, such as rolls (Cold, but we note Hot, if offered), tails, mac & cheese, and simply "lobsters" for those with steamed, boiled, grilled, or stuffed lobsters. Email any updates you want to see included to: **Publisher@QTPublishing.com**.
Keep in mind that while some of these establishments are full-service, year-round restaurants, others are seasonal or only offer lobster items "in season."
 Some smaller, cherished lobster shacks may be BYOB; some are cash only. Always check ahead to avoid disappointment AND love lobster as the locals do!

💋MAINE

Arundel Wharf Seafood	Kennebunkport	ArundelWharf.com
Bagaduce Lunch	Penobscot	Facebook.com/Bagaduce
Barnacle Billy's	Ogunquit	BarnBilly.com
Beal's Lobster Pier	Southwest Harbor	BealsLobster.com
Becky's Diner	Portland	BeckysDiner.com
Bite into Maine	Cape Elizabeth	BiteIntoMaine.com
Bob's Clam Hut	Kittery	BobsClamHut.com
Boone's Fish House & Oyster Room	Portland	BoonesFishHouse.com
Boothbay Lobster Wharf	Boothbay Harbor	BoothbayLobsterWharf.com
C-Ray Lobster	Bar Harbor	C-RayLobster.com
Cameron's Lobster House	Brunswick	CameronsLobsterHouse.com

Cape Neddick Lobster Pound & Harborside Restaurant	Cape Neddick	CapeNeddick.com
Cape Pier Chowder House	Kennebunkport	CapePorpoiseLobster.com
Captain Hook's Take Out	Wells	CaptainHooksTakeOut.com
The Chart Room	Bar Harbor	ChartRoomBarHarbor.com
Chauncy Creek Lobster Pier	Kittery Point	ChauncyCreek.co
The Clam Shack	Kennebunk	TheClamShack.net
Claws	Rockland	ClawsRocklandMaine.com
Cook's Lobster & Ale House	Barley Island	CooksLobster.com
Day's Crabmeat & Lobster	Yarmouth	DaysCrabmeatAndLobster.com
DiMillo's on the Water	Portland	DiMillos.com
East Boothbay General Store	East Boothbay	EBGS.us
Estes Lobster House	Harpswell	EstesLobsterHouse.com
Eventide Oyster Co.	Portland	EventideOysterCo.com
Five Islands Lobster Co.	Georgetown	FiveIslandsLobster.com
Footbridge Lobster	Ogunquit	Facebook.com/Footbridge-Lobster
Galyn's	Bar Harbor	GalynsBarHarbor.com
Harraseeket Lunch & Lobster Co.	South Freeport	HarraseeketLunchAndLobster.com
The Highroller Lobster Co.	Portland	TheHighRoller.me
Hobbs Harborside Restaurant	Wells	HobbsHarborside.com
Johnson's Seafood & Steak	North Berwick	EatAtJohnsons.com
Jonathan's Ogunquit	Ogunquit	JonathansOgunquit.com
Kaler's Restaurant	Boothbay Harbor	KalersLobsters.com
Lobster Claw Pound & Restaurant	Saco	LobsterClawMaine.com
Lobster Cooker	Freeport	TheLobsterCooker.com
Lobster Cove	York	LobsterCoveRestaurant.com
Lobster Dock	Boothbay Harbor	TheLobsterDock.com
Lobster in the Rough	York	TheRoughYorkMaine.com
Lobster Shack at Two Lights	Cape Elizabeth	LobsterShackTwoLights.com
Lobsterman's Wharf	East Boothbay	LobstermansWharf.com
Lord's Clam Box	Wells	LordsClamBox.com
Luke's at Tenants Harbor	St. George	LukesLobster.com
Lunt's Gateway Lobster Pound	Trenton	LuntsGatewayLobster.com
Mabel's Lobster Claw	Kennebunkport	MabelsLobster.com
Mack's Place	Bridgton	MacksPlaceRestaurant.com
The Maine Diner	Wells	MaineDiner.com

McLoon's Lobster Shack	South Thomaston	McLoonsLobster.com
McSeagull's Restaurant	Boothbay Harbor	McSeagullsOnline.com
Millers Lobster Company	Spruce Head	MillersLobster.com
Muscongus Bay Lobster	Round Pond	MaineFreshLobster.com
Nubb's Lobster Shack	Cape Neddick	DestinationHotels.com/Cliff-House/dining
Nunan's Lobster Hut	Kennebunkport	NunansLobsterHut.com
Oarweed Oceanside Restaurant	Ogunquit	Oarweed.com
Ogunquit Lobster Pound	Ogunquit	OgunquitLobsterPound.com
Perkin's Cove Lobster Shack	Ogunquit	Lobster-Shack.com
Perry's Lobster Shack	Surry	PerrysLobsterShack.com
The Porthole	Portland	PortholeMaine.com
Portland Lobster Company	Portland	PortlandLobsterCompany.com
Red's Eats	Wiscasset	RedsEatsMaine.com
Rising Tide Restaurant	Scarborough	RisingTideRestaurant.com
Robinson's Wharf	Southport	Robinsons-Wharf.com
Rooster's Roadhouse	Bethel	RoostersRoadhouse.com
Robert's Maine Grill	Kittery	RobertsMaineGrill.com
Scarborough Fish & Lobster	Scarborough	ScarboroughLobster.com
Sea Salt Lobster Restaurant	Saco	SeaSaltLobsterRestaurant.com
Shannon's Unshelled	Boothbay Harbor	ShannonsUnshelled.biz
Sprague's Lobster	Wiscasset	Facebook.com/SpraguesLobster
Stewman's Lobster Pound	Bar Harbor	StewmansLobsterPound.com
Taste of Maine Restaurant	Woolrich	TasteOfMaine.com
Thurston's Lobster Pound	Bernard	ThurstonForLobster.com
Trenton Bridge Lobster Pound	Trenton	TrentonBridgeLobster.com
Warren's Lobster House	Kittery	LobsterHouse.com
Weathervane Seafood Restaurant	Kittery	WeathervaneSeafoods.com
Wells Beach Lobster Pound	Wells Beach	WellsBeachLobster.com
Young's Lobster Pound	Belfast	Facebook.com/YoungsLobsterPound/

NEW HAMPSHIRE

401 Tavern	Hampton	401Tavern.com
Ackerly's Grill and Galley	Alton	AckerlysGrillandGalleyRestaurant.com
Al's Seafood	North Hampton	AlsSeafoodNH.com
Angelina's Ristorante Italiano	Concord	AngelinasRestaurant.com
The Beach Plum	(several)	LobsterRolls.com
BG's Boat House Restaurant	Portsmouth	BGsBoatHouse.com
Blue Bistro	Laconia	Naswa.com/Blue-Bistro
Blue Latitudes	Dover	BlueLatitudes.net
Bolton's Lake House	Kingston	BoltonsLakeHouse.com
The Breakers at the Ashworth	Hampton Beach	AshworthHotel.com/Dining
Brown's Lobster Pound	Seabrook	BrownsLobsterPound.com
Bubba's Bar & Grille	Newbury	BubbasBarAndGrille.com
Buckley's Great Steaks	Merrimack	BuckleysGreatSteaks.com
Canoe	(several)	MagicFoodRestaurantGroup.com
Clam Haven	Derry	ClamHaven.com
Common Man	(several)	TheCMan.com
Corner House Inn	Sandwich	CornerHouseInn.com
Cotton	Manchester	CottonFood.com
Dipsy Doodle Dairy Bar	Northfield	DipsyDoodle.com
The Food Shack	Epping	TheFoodShackNH.com
Geno's Chowder & Sandwich Shop	Portsmouth	GenosChowder.com
George's Seafood & BBQ	Plymouth	GeorgesSeafood.com
Gordi's Fish & Steak House	Lincoln	GordisFishAndSteak.com
Hanover Street Chophouse	Manchester	HanoverStreetChophouse.com
Hooked Seafood	Manchester	HookedOnIgnite.com
Jake's Seafood & Grill	West Ossipee	JakesSeafoodCo.com
Jena's Lobster Quest	Ossipee	Singlepage.com/Jenas-Lobster-Quest
Jesse's Steak and Seafood	Hanover	Jesses.com
Jimmy Jones Locker	Rochester	JimmyJonesLocker.net
Johnson's Seafood & Steak	(several)	EatAtJohnsons.com
Jumpin' Jay's Fish Café	Portsmouth	JumpinJays.com
Justin's Seafood Hut	Rye	Facebook.com/JustinsSeafoodHut
Lakehouse Grille	Meredith	TheCMan.com
Lavinia's	Center Harbor	LaviniasDining.com
The Little Red Schoolhouse	Campton	LittleRedSchoolhouseNH.com

Lobster Boat Restaurant	(several)	LobsterBoatRestaurant.com
Lobster Claw II	Derry	LobsterClaw2.com
Lobster Q Seafood & BBQ	Hampstead	Facebook.com/LobsterQ
Lobster Tail Restaurant & Lounge	Windham	LobsterTail.net
Lobster Trap	North Conway	LobsterTrapRestaurant.com
Makris Lobster & Steakhouse	Concord	EatALobster.com
Markey's Lobster Pool	Seabrook	MarkeysLobsterPool.com
Morrissey's Front Porch	Wolfeboro	MorrisseysFrontPorch.com
Mount Washington Hotel & Resort	Bretton Woods	OmniHotels.com
NazBar	Laconia	Naswar.com/Naz-Bar-Grill
Newick's Lobster House	Dover, Concord	Newicks.com
The New Woodshed Restaurant	Moultonborough	NewWoodshed.com
O'Steak and Seafood	Laconia, Concord	MagicFoodRestaurantGroup.com
Petey's Summertime Seafood	Rye	Peteys.com
Poor Boys Diner	Londonderry	PoorBoysDiner.com
Poor People's Pub	Sanbornville	PoorPeoplesPub.com
Purple Tomato Farmers Market	Lincoln	Facebook.com/PurpleTomatoFarmersMarket
Ray's Seafood	Rye	RaysSeafoodRestaurant.com
Red Fox Bar & Grille	Jackson	RedFoxBarAndGrille.com
River House	Portsmouth	RiverHouse53Bow.com
Row 34	Portsmouth	Row34.NH.com
Rye Harbor Lobster Pound	Rye Harbor	Facebook.com/RyeHarborLobsterPound
Sandy Point Restaurant	Alton Bay	Facebook.com/SandyPointAlton
Sawyer's Dairy Bar	Gilford	SawyersNH.com
Shibley's at the Pier	Alton Bay	ShibleysAtThePier.com
Shovel Handle Pub	Jackson	ShovelHandlePub.com
Surf	Nashua, Portsmouth	SurfSeafood.com
Tamarack	Weirs Beach	GlobeEater.com/TamarackWeirsBeach
Town Docks Restaurant	Meredith	TheCMan.com
The Tuckaway Tavern	Raymond	TheTuckaway.com
Villaggio Ristorante	Manchester	VillaggioNH.com
Walter's Basin Pub	Holderness	WaltersBasin.com
Weathervane Seafood Restaurant	(several)	WeathervaneSeafoods.com
Wolfetrap Grill & Raw Bar	Wolfeboro	WolfetrapGrillAndRawBar.com
XO on Elm	Manchester	XOonElm.com
The Yard	Manchester	Facebook.com/The-Yard-Restaurant

OTHER GREAT FINDS:

7 Seas Restaurant & Pub	Milford, CT	7SeasMilford.com
Abbott's Lobster in the Rough	Noank, CT	AbbottsLobster.com
Alive and Kicking Lobsters	Cambridge, MA	AliveAndKickingLobsters.com
Alonzo & Berlin's Lobster House	Key West, FL	AAndBLobsterHouse.com
Anthony's Seafood	Middletown, RI	AnthonysSeafood.net
Arnold's Lobster & Clam Bar	Eastham, MA	ArnoldsRestaurant.com
B&G Oysters	Boston, MA	BandGOysters.com
The Barking Crab	Boston, MA	BarkingCrab.com
The Bayside Restaurant	Westport, MA	TheBaysideRestaurant.com
The Beachcomber	Wellfleet, MA	TheBeachcomber.com
Belle Isle Seafood	Winthrop, MA	BelleIsleSeafood.com
Big Fin Seafood Kitchen	Orlando, FL	BigFinSeafood.com
Blue Lobster	Berlin, CT	BlueLobsterSeafood.com
Bob Lobster Company	Newbury, MA	BobLobster.com
Bostonia Public House	Boston, MA	BostoniaPublicHouse.com
Brick Alley Pub	Newport, RI	BrickAlley.com
The Capital Grille	(coast-to-coast)	CapitalGrille.com
Captain Scott's	Sandwich, MA	CaptainScotts.com
Champlin's Seafood Deck	Narragansett, RI	Champlins.com
The Clam Bake	Fort Myers, FL	ClamBakeFortMyers.com
The Clam Bar	Amagansett, NY	ClamBarHamptons.com
Claudio's Restaurant	Greenport, NY	Claudios.com
The Dolphin	Natick, MA	DolphinSeafood.com
Dolphin Tiki Bar & Grill	Marco Island, FL	DolphinTiki.com
Ed's Lobster Bar	Manhattan, NY	LobsterBarNYC.com
Evelyn's Nanaquaket Drive-In	Iverton, RI	EvelynsDriveIn.com
Ford's Lobster	Noank, CT	FordsLobster.com
Hemenway's	Providence, RI	HemenwaysRestaurant.com
Hingham Lobster Pound	Hingham, MA	HinghamLobster.com
Iggy's Boardwalk	Warwick, RI	IggysBoardwalk.com
Island Creek Oyster Bar	Boston, MA	IslandCreekOysterBar.com
James Hook and Company	Boston, MA	JamesHookLobster.com
Jazzy's Mainely Lobster	Cocoa Beach, FL	JazzysMainelyLobster.com
Joe Fish Seafood Restaurant	(several), MA	JoeFish.net
Johnny Ad's Drive-In	Old Saybrook, CT	JohnnyAds.com

Jordan Lobster Farms	Island Park, NY	JordanLobsterFarms.com
Kimball Farm	(several), MA	KimballFarm.com
Larsen's Fish Market	Martha's Vineyard, MA	LarsensFishMarket.com
Lazy Lobster	Sarasota, FL	SarasotaLazyLobster.com
Lobster Barn	Abington, MA	LobsterBarn.net
The Lobster Claw	Orleans, MA	LobsterClaw.com
Lobster Haven	Tampa, FL	LobsterHaven.net
Lobster Landing	Clinton, CT	Facebook.com/LobsterLanding
The Lobster Pool	Rockport, MA	TheLobsterPool.com
Lobster Pot Restaurant	Sarasota, FL	SarasotaLobsterPot.com
The Lobster Roll	Amagansett, NY	LobsterRoll.com
Lobster Shack	Seaford, NY	LobsterShackLongIsland.com
The Lobster Shanty	Salem, MA	LobsterShantySalem.com
The Lobster Stop	Quincy, MA	TheLobsterStop.net
Lobster Trap Restaurant	Bourne, MA	LobsterTrap.net
Mac's Seafood	(several), MA	MacsSeafood.com
Menemsha Fish Market	Martha's Vineyard, MA	MenemshaFishMarket.net
The Mill Wharf Restaurant	Scituate, MA	MillWharf.com
Neptune Oyster House	Boston, MA	NeptuneOyster.com
Newport Lobster Shack	Newport, RI	NewportLobsterShack.com
Nick's Lobster House	Brooklyn, NY	NicksLobsterHouse.com
The Palm	Boston, MA & NYC	ThePalm.com
Paradise Seafood	Marco Island, FL	ParadiseSeafoodMarco.com
Periwinkles Restaurant	Essex, MA	PeriwinklesRestaurant.com
PJ's Lobster House	Port Jefferson, NY	PJLobsterHouse.com
Providence Oyster Bar	Providence, RI	ProvOysterBar.com
Red Hook Lobster Pound	(several), NY	RedHookLobster.com
Riverway Lobster House	South Yarmouoth, MA	RiverwayLobsterHouseRestaurant.com
Roy Moore Lobster Co.	Rockport, MA	Facebook.com/Roy-Moore-Lobster-Co
Snug Harbor Fish Company	Duxbury, MA	SnugHarborFishCompany.com
Tommy Doyle's	Brockton, Easton, MA	TommyDoylesPub.com
Tony's Clam Shop	Quincy, MA	TonysClamShop.com
Westbrook Lobster Restaurant	(several)	WestbrookLobster.com
Woods Seafood	Plymouth, MA	WoodsSeafoods.com
Yankee Lobster Company	Boston, MA	YankeeLobsterCompany.com

Just the way I like it... Lobaciously Super Simple!

LOBACIOUS NOTABLE QUOTABLES

"I did 12 shows in 13 weeks at a summer theatre in Maine where we were paid $35 a week. After taxes and $25 for room and board, I had enough money for a pack of cigarettes and a bowl of lobster bisque."
-- Martin Landau (1928 - 2017)
American actor

"A lobster bisque ought to be the crowning glory of the potager. Silky as the gigolo's compliment and fishy as a chancellor's promise."
-- A.A. Gill (1954 – 2016)
British travel & food writer & critic

"A woman shall never be seen eating or drinking, unless it be lobster salad and champagne."
-- Lord Byron (1788 - 1824)
English poet & playwright

"Grilling outside with my parents at the Jersey shore, we would grill lobster and corn in the summer."
-- Bobby Flay (1964 -)
American celebrity chef

"The world is my lobster."
-- Keith O'Neill (1976 -)
Irish footballer

"Books… are like lobster shells. We surround ourselves with 'em, then we grow out of 'em and leave 'em behind, as evidence of our earlier stages of development."
-- Dorothy L. Sayers (1893 – 1957)
English writer & poet

"When Life gives you lemons, order the lobster tail."

-- Ziad K. Abdelnour
Author of "Economic Warfare"

"If a lobster didn't look like a sci-fi monster, people would be less able to drop him alive into boiling water."

-- George Carlin (1937 – 2008)
American comedian

"I do not understand why, when I ask for a grilled lobster in a restaurant, I'm never served a cooked telephone."

-- Salvador Dali (1904 – 1989)
Spanish artist

"There is not one woman born who does not like Red Lobster cheddar biscuits. Anyone who claims otherwise is a liar and a socialist."

-- Tina Fey (1970 -)
American actress & comedian

"He looks much more like a lobster than most lobsters do."

-- P.G. Wodehouse (1881 – 1975)
English author & humorist

"The proper place to eat a lobster… is in a lobster shack as close to the sea as possible. There is no menu card because there is nothing else to eat except boiled lobster with melted butter."

-- Pearl S. Buck (1892 – 1973)
American novelist

"Lobster's one of the only animals that have to put up with being alive in the restaurant. If you go to a steakhouse, folks – no cow tank."

-- Richard Jeni (1957 – 2007)
American comedian

Photo courtesy of Henry Perks

Author's Acknowledgements

Though they insist that this was a labor of love and pleasure, I thank everyone who has served as a taste tester for these recipes as they were in development over the years. I especially thank my mother, Glenna Gulumian Burnham, for instilling in me a great taste for lobster!

Also, although most of the photographs are my own, I offer special thanks and appreciation to the following for some of their photographs: Robert Burnham, David diVeroli, Brooke Lark, Jeffrey Larrabee, Francis MacDonald, Ron Martin, Henry Perk, Steven Raichen, and Herson Rodriguez.

Glenna Burnham

About the Author

A professional voiceover artist, Cathy Burnham Martin narrates her own books as well as those by other authors. Her Audiobooks appear on sites like Audible.com, as well as Amazon and iTunes. In addition to fiction, nonfiction, and cookbooks, Cathy writes articles for the *GoodLiving123.com* blog. A member of Actors Equity and the National Speakers Association for 20+ years, she is a motivational speaker dubbed *"The Morale Booster,"* a corporate communications geek, dedicated foodie, and award-winning journalist. A former news anchor and talk show host, she wrote, produced, and hosted dozens of documentaries, TV specials, and news reports, ranging from the Moscow Super Power Summit and the opening of the Berlin Wall to NH's First-in-the-Nation Presidential Primaries. Since her Dad received chef training at the famed Boston Copley Plaza, and her Mom became the "Best Cook in Town," Cathy's "need to feed" launched food coverage on WMUR-TV, New Hampshire's ABC affiliate, long before food channels emerged. She also managed a community access TV station, continues to review restaurants and events, and is a top reviewer for Trip Advisor online.

Beyond cookbooks, her additional writing credits include 300+ episodes of *New Hampshire Minutes*, plus authoring books, including:
- **The Bimbo Has Brains… and Other Freaky Facts**
- **A Dangerous Book for Dogs: How to Train Your Human**
- **Healthy Thinking Habits: 7 Attitude Skills Simplified**
- **Of the Same Blood: Your Eurasian Heritage**
- **The Miles-Mannered Man**, a whimsical collection of tall tales, wagging tails, & tantalizing treats

www.ingramcontent.com/pod-product-compliance
Lightning Source LLC
Chambersburg PA
CBHW041535220426
43663CB00002B/46